Bearing Witness

Eight weeks in Palestine

Ana Barahona

Metete Publications
Pictures and text © 2011 Ana Barahona
More pictures can be viewed at: https://network23.org/ana
ISBN: 978-1-908099-00-6
Cover: graffiti outside a Palestinian school in Hebron.
Back cover: Palestinian girl at her home door, observing the Israeli kids next door.

All the names in the text have been shortened and changed.
To obtain more copies of this book: abarahona@riseup.net

Acknowledgements

First and foremost I need to thank every one in Palestine and in Britain that made my visit to Palestine possible. I believe it is safer for them to remain unnamed.

Then I should thank every one who has collaborated in the writing, and encouraged and helped me in the editing and publishing of this diary: Jordi, Chris, Ted, Sharron, Gavin, Jon, Tony, Mark and my mother.

Contents

PROLOGUE

I have been hoping to go to Palestine for quite a while now. Not that I have ever felt attracted to the Palestinian issue or the Arab culture. As a woman, I profoundly disapprove of the social ostracism women seem to be relegated to in most Arabic cultures, and would only travel to one of those countries with a group of people I could trust.

But I remember when, as a child, I watched the news on TV about a "conflict" in the "Middle East", "Palestinian Territories" "Holy Land"... and I thought, what a shame, it is Holy Land and they are fighting. I thought that precisely there, in Holy Land people should not fight, or have a war. Moreover, how could we Christians go there as pilgrims?

As I grew up I read more about the subject. I only read whatever would fall into my hands at first, with no special interest. And later, more and more outraged, I would think, "what are we 'the rich from the first world' doing about this?"

And then Rachel Corrie was killed. Her writings were published in "The Guardian", including emails she had sent to her family. What she said about the Palestinians' situation did not surprise me any more, but that was the way I learnt that anyone can go to Palestine and help. Anyone, even me. Only going on my own was completely out of the question.

1

PREPARATIONS

A. tells me that he is travelling to Palestine in a few weeks. He was there a few months ago, and on that occasion I asked him to tell me with a bit more notice the next time he decided to go. And here he is, telling me with enough notice that he is going again for a few months. So I think I should take this chance to go not entirely on my own.

I suggest that we travel together but A. quickly dismisses the idea. He first explains that the Israeli occupation means that it is Israel border authorities we have to deal with before entering Palestine. The Israeli state considers all Palestinians a terrorism threat, and by extension, any one who supports the Palestinian cause. Therefore the Israeli authorities will not allow entry to the country to any one who is suspected of supporting the Palestinian cause. So if we want to make sure we are allowed in the country once we have arrived at the airport, the Israeli authorities will need to be satisfied that we are not a threat. If we arrive together, they will put us in separate rooms and interrogate us looking for contradictions between his story and mine, so it is a lot safer if we just arrive on different days.

FIRST WEEK

First Monday - **Jerusalem**

I arrive at Tel Aviv airport at around five o'clock in the morning. There is a shuttle service to Jerusalem from the airport. It consists of a van that functions like a shared taxi, with seats and some space for suitcases. It leaves the airport only when all the seats are occupied, and each person pays their fare when they arrive at their destination.

On the way to Jerusalem the palm trees grab my attention. There are lots of them, all lined up alongside the road. Once in Jerusalem, the whiteness of the houses strikes me. All around Jerusalem, both in the outskirts and in the centre, old and new houses are all built with clean white stone, and all the stones are of the same size. Even the city wall is made of that kind of stone, just like any other building.

Perhaps because I am the only foreigner, or perhaps because I am the only one going to the Old City, I am the last one to leave the taxi. We arrive at the hostel at around nine o'clock.

As the taxi stops in front of my hostel, a man approaches us, asking what we are after. When I mention the hostel where I am staying he says he works there and helps me with my cases. After finding a room and paying for it, he offers to show me Jerusalem. I tell him that all I want now is a shop where I can buy some food and he answers that he can show me all the cheap food stores. I am dying to take off my shoes and rest, but thinking that we will be out only for a short time, I leave my things there and go out to meet him quickly, to avoid wasting his time. Big mistake: time, or my concept of it, does not seem to exist for people here.

He takes me along the streets of the Old City. In the map they look like normal streets, but in reality they are mostly pedestrian, full of steps, hills and shops that literally jut out into the street. None of them have any food to sell, and before I realise, we are in the church of the Holy Sepulchre, which I am both glad and dismayed to see - I had asked this man to just show me a food shop! He is acting as a tourist guide and I am feeling my feet burning after my twelve hour journey.

He takes me around the church until my need for a rest is big enough to stop him. I make it clear to him that what I really want is to get lost on my own in the

3

city, but not now. Above all, and urgently, I need to have some food, take off my shoes and sleep.

He then takes me to a bakery where there is only a man taking pita bread in and out of an oven. There is no counter and no till. It looks more like a workshop. My "guide" insists that I buy a piece of bread covered with herbs and spices and I almost have to get angry to get just two pieces of plain bread. I ask my "guide" how to say "thank you" and he says: "sukran". I say sukran to the baker and the "guide" goes on talking and says he is Palestinian.

I get rid of him at last and I go on my own to a little shop that I have seen before and buy oil and milk. With these goods I go to my room to have breakfast and sleep. But for some reason I can not manage to sleep so I get up, put my sandals on and go out to the street - I should now tell my friends and family that I have arrived safe and sound.

There is a computer in the vestibule of the hostel for guests to access the internet. I ask about the conditions of use and, while I am there, I ask about telephone cards too. The boy at the desk tells me about a particular shop outside the wall, and I head over there. I spend about an hour walking around with no result: I do not find a single telephone card shop. However, it is a good exercise for me to get to know a bit of the outside part of the wall, and what seems to be the most westernised part of the city, judging from the type of shops.

Back in the Old City I go to the Christian Information Centre, but it is closed. There is a notice on the door with the schedule of all the masses and services available from the different Christian sects all over Jerusalem, and in which language they are. I make a note of my nearest catholic church. From there I head to the touristy shop where one can exchange money and buy mobile phones and other electronic things.

A tradesman from another shop approaches me inviting me to enter his own shop.

"Sorry, I can't", I say. "I am in a hurry to buy a telephone card."

"Oh I wait until you finish", he says. It takes me some twenty minutes to buy two phone cards, one for local calls and another for international calls. I had imagined that the good man would have given up the waiting by now, but when I come out there he is, standing outside, waiting for me. I say:

"I am sorry, I need to find a telephone now."

"You can call from my shop, come I'll show you."

I follow him to his shop, and once there he bids me sit down on a chair and offers me some tea. I refuse because what I want to do is make a phone call. He insists that this is just his hospitality and "I have" to drink something. He introduces me to his son, of some twelve years of age, who seems to take care of the shop when his father leaves to look for customers, and he leaves. After ten minutes of forced conversation, I tell the son that, if his father does not appear in five minutes, I am going to leave, because I do have an urgent call to make.

4

After another ten minutes, the father appears, talks to his son in a language that I believe is Arabic, and after a few more minutes, he looks at me and says:

"You wanted your tea, isn't it?"

I tell him that I do not want any tea, that I have come to his shop because he told me that I could make a phone call from here, but obviously that is not true, so I need to leave because I am in a hurry. He says something quickly and with the best of my smiles I tell him, already from outside the shop:

"No, it's all right, thank you."

I sense him saying something behind me and I run away from there, quite annoyed and with my lesson learnt: the "no thank you" must be given before they have had the chance to get you to visit their shop. I go back to the hostel to make my phone calls and I dutifully tell my friends and family that I have arrived safe and sound.

Now I do go to sleep. When I wake up I decide to set off for the church, which is right next to a small esplanade that looks like a car park. To get to the entrance I need to go round a barrier that acts as a gate for cars. I expect to be asked to stop by security guards next to this gate but they just say a mute "hello" and let me into this esplanade, and then into the church.

Once inside this building with the aspect of a Romanesque church - but with perfectly cut white stone, just as every other building - I find myself in the foyer of a hotel. The mass is celebrated in a chapel on the upper floor, access to which is through some lateral stairs. The chapel is all white, and the walls have that characteristic stone too. There are no benches, only wickerwork chairs, also white, all stuck together, leaving a walkway in the middle, so the sensation is that of any catholic church.

After mass I approach the priest to talk to him. He explains that the whole estate is the property of the Vatican State, so this piece of land is diplomatically immune territory and police can only enter with permission.

I tell him I was in the Holy Sepulchre this morning and that I did not really like it, among other reasons, because of the architectural structures around it. They reminded me more of the crusades and the Middle Ages, and about the present divisions between the different churches, than of any trace of the epoch of Jesus. Besides, there is no time or space to pray, at least at the sepulchre. It is a very small cave and the queues are long, so it is not appropriate to stay for longer than five minutes, and those are not proper conditions.

He says there are various reasons why most buildings on the Holy Sites are dated after the year 300 CE. The destruction of Jerusalem in the year 125 CE was even more brutal and destructive than the one in the year 70 CE; the Romans left no "stone on stone". And Christians did not have the economical or political power to build in such places then. Moreover, marking the exact places where things had happened was not considered so important because it was well known where each event took place through oral tradition. Neither was it so important to leave things for posterity, since those Christians were expecting to see the end of times within their own lifetimes.

First Tuesday - **Guns and soldiers**

The outside noise and light wake me up at around seven o'clock in the morning. When I go out to buy some breakfast, the attentive sir who wanted to be my tourist guide yesterday spots me and asks where I am going and whether I know my way. I say I do, thank you very much, I turn round and I go on walking. I hear him say:

"Ok, when you come back, we'll do something today."

His English is not perfect so I guess that what he means is that he wants to be my tourist guide. I turn to him briefly, not knowing whether to laugh or cry. I do not have the patience to send him to hell politely so I just move my head and leave. I would love to share with this Palestinian my story and my reasons for being here, but I can not risk being reported to the Israeli authorities by some one who knows where I am staying this week.

Once back in the hostel I ask around the other guests where they buy their food, as there is a communal kitchen where we can cook. They mention a fruit and vegetable market outside Damascus Gate. They also recommend me to walk there, using the pedestrian streets in the Old City, inside the wall, as a way of sightseeing the city while getting there.

I then go to the Muslim Quarter through the Old City as a full-time tourist. I buy a piece of bread with spices. They are not spices but a kind of dust that tastes like aromatic herbs and looks like dusty fodder. I now understand why "my guide" wanted to convince me to buy the spiced bread: two normal pieces of pita bread cost one shekel, while just one with the green dust costs four. The mix of herbs and dust also has some olive oil and they heat it for you, so it looks healthy, feels warm and fills the stomach.

I eat it as I walk and I end up in Via Dolorosa, which is also full of shops, and from there to a street that, according to my map, goes straight to Damascus Gate. The closer I get to the Gate, the more crowded it gets. The men have beards and Palestinian handkerchiefs on their heads, called "kheffiyeh", like Arafat used to wear. The women wear dark tunics from head to toe. Some of them have their faces covered too.

As I walk, the crowd becomes more like a multitude with little space between one person and the next, but suddenly a young man in western clothes stands out, at least to my eyes. He is not wearing anything on his head; he does not have a beard. He is wearing a white western shirt and black western trousers. He clearly stands out of the crowd. I am not sure if it is his clothes that have made me stare at him for a fraction of a second or if it is the thing hanging from his shoulder that he is grabbing with his hand. Time has stopped between this guy and me for that fraction of a second. I look down to see the black tool he is holding. His finger is out holding a trigger and I realise it is a machine gun. At least I know it is a weapon, black and very modern, much more sophisticated than anything else I have ever seen in films or in the news.

No one has stopped or even noticed. We all continue walking and time recovers its usual pace.

I try to follow my map in order to get to Damascus Gate and the market there. However at the end of the street there are a few turns and I end up in streets that go up and down all the time, all made of stone steps, all quite solitary, and I realise that I am lost.

As I turn round a corner I see four Israeli soldiers, dressed in green camou-flage uniforms, talking to an Arabic-looking boy. The soldiers have machine guns hanging from their shoulders. The boy is unarmed. Four armed soldiers, one unarmed boy, a deserted street. As I walk away, I wonder if, for a split second, I did not see a ray of desperation in the boy's eyes. I continue walking the unpaved streets and climbing steps up and down as I go along.

Suddenly at the top of some steps I need to stop to give way to a row of school girls, with their teacher behind them. I look for the teacher in front of them but there is none. Instead, there is a man with a weapon hanging from his shoulder too. Then I remember some piece of news some time ago talking about the need to protect Jewish school girls so that they can go to school safely. We are in the Muslim Quarter.

Fig 1: Loophole in the wall

At last I begin to hear some traffic noise. That means I am very near a gate, but I suspect it is not Damascus Gate. I go out through this gate and there is a corridor formed by mobile fruit shops. I do my shopping and I ask what gate this is. This is Herod's Gate. Damascus Gate is the next one down the street. I walk in the direction that the stall keeper has told me, get to Damascus Gate, walk through it back into the Old City

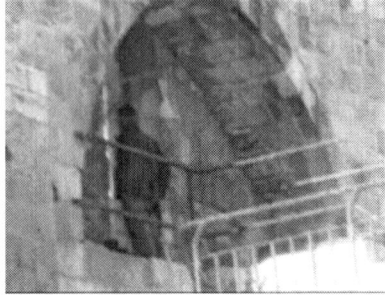

Fig 2: Loophole over Damascus Gate

and realise how I got lost and why: there is no indication, not even the name of the streets to look them up on the map.

As at Herod's Gate, the market here is made up of two rows of stands that form a kind of aisle that ends up at the gate; only this one is a lot longer than the one at Herod's Gate and the stalls are bigger too. And of course the crowd is now as dense as when I was approaching Damascus Gate from the other side.

Near the street where I got lost there are some toilets. The gents toilets are at street level, besides some shops. The ladies toilets are next to the wall, at the height of it, after climbing about fifty steps. Just outside the ladies toilets there is a stone sitting space. The view is very pretty: I can see the roofs of the houses, and the wall of the city from the inside.

There are some loopholes in the stone where I would imagine ancient soldiers would sit with their bows and arrows defending the city. Fig 1

The one over the gate is bigger than the rest, and bigger than a door. There is a soldier with a machine gun looking out to the outside part of the gate. Fig 2

I go down to the street and out again through Damascus Gate. Right on top of the gate is the loophole where I saw the soldier with his machine gun before. From where he is, he can see the whole esplanade, where there is a crowd in a festive and colourful atmosphere. Fig 3

I enter the gate again and it is even more crowded now. I continue walking, trying to find the Church of the Holy Sepulchre, but I only manage to go round in too many circles. A group of Italians are praying the Via Crucis with their priest, stopping at each station, praying and singing. They are a tourist attraction themselves. I decide to follow them because I know that the Via Crucis will end up at the Church of the Holy Sepulchre, which is where I want to go.

Once they reach the church and finish praying, they stop being traditional pilgrims to become very modern tourists. I get ready to take some pictures too. I look into my bag and I realise that my photo camera has been stolen. I continue "working" with the video camera trying not to think too much of the stolen one.

Once I get out of the church I see that A. has sent me a text message: he is here in Jerusalem, and he is now at his hostel having a rest. I get out of the small street system in a hurry to go and see him.

A.'s hostel is a lot busier than mine. A. is actually on his way out when I arrive, and we are just two of the many people going up and down the stairs. He introduces me to a couple of people as his friends and they leave, allowing me to stay inside waiting for them. I grab a book from a shelf and read until some Spanish guy comes and talks to me. He is a volunteer working in a Palestinian village and he is here just having a rest from it all, like A. and his friends. They come back and we all talk together.

A. wants to go back to Ramallah tomorrow and suggests that I go with him. His friends say it will be very difficult to travel tomorrow and advise him to leave it for the day after tomorrow. He says he will do that, and he will call me and we will go together.

Fig 3: Damascus Gate.

First Wednesday - **Majestic Jerusalem**

A. has left Jerusalem on his own and I stay doing some more tourism. I head for the Mount of Zion, to the South of Jerusalem, looking for David's Tomb and the Cenacle. I get lost in a park and I find a stone building in the middle of the forest, with an open door at its base. I wonder what such an open house is doing in the middle of nowhere and it turns out it is the back entrance (or one of them) to the complex of the Tomb of David.

What is supposed to be David's tomb is divided in two parts by a panel, so that one half is visited by men only and the other half is visited by women only, making sure we do not mix up.

The Cenacle, or "Room of the Last Supper", is a room upstairs, in another building after walking through a few gardens. We are told that Jesus appeared in front of his disciples here too, once resurrected, that Pentecost happened here and that the first Church was born and lived here too.

All these places I have visited are not too much about religion but very much about tourism. They are not places where I feel invited to pray. There is too much traffic of tourists who, coming for just a few days, only have time to arrive, queue while taking loudly in social conversation, enter, take the picture and leave; where is the next attraction please.

In any case, and now that I am here, I continue with my own "tour". There is a memorial for the victims of the Holocaust in the same complex of gardens, yards and buildings. It is just a little room all made of white stone, like everything else here. An old man offers candles to visitors in exchange for a donation and there is a kind of altar at eye-level. It is small; just big enough to put candles inside without getting the stone black with the smoke. Nothing more. I light a candle for all victims of all holocausts and leave - next attraction please.

I explore all the paths that I have not seen yet and I end up in a car park with huge coaches in it. I follow the road that those coaches must have used to get here, bordering the city wall. The road bends down the hill and goes alongside the city wall. In some places the space between the road and the wall is so narrow I end up walking on the rampart to stay clear of the cars.

I come up to the end of this road into what looks like a police control, right before accessing the Esplanade of the Temple and the Wailing Wall. Almost everyone entering has their head covered. Most, if not all, are orthodox Jewish, with their black cloaks and hats. I slow down discreetly waiting to see some tour-ists. I do not want to risk being stopped for being a woman in trousers with an uncovered head and a camera. When I see that they allow a small group of tour-ists with their cameras hanging from their necks and nothing on their heads, I go after them. Again, men use one entrance and women use another one. Our bags are searched and we go through beeping gates.

Once inside, there is a big sign as big as a road traffic sign, with the rules of behaviour for all to read. From that moment on and during the rest of the day I see armed people everywhere, some in military uniforms with normal machine guns, others in plain clothes with strange weapons. But people just ignore them. It seems they are conscious that those weapons are there to protect the crowd from any potential attack, unlike at Damascus Gate, where the weapons are ready for use against the Arab crowd.

The Temple Esplanade is divided and clearly delimited into different areas. Half of it, furthest away from the Wall, is where every one is allowed, and is therefore the part with the biggest crowd of tourists. It has little interest for the Jewish people who come here for religious reasons. Then there is the other half, closer to the wall, used for prayer and mourning. This part is itself divided in two. One huge extension, on the left hand side facing the wall, is for Jewish men only. The last bit, the tiniest area of all, is for women. It is just a small corner, on the right hand side, facing the wall.

It is said that this Wailing Wall is the only thing remaining from the "Second Temple", which was built on the ruins of the one built by Solomon. Officially, it is called the West Wall of that temple. This clashes with the version of History that says that the Romans did not leave "stone on stone" the second time they destroyed this temple.

On the other side of the wall, where the original Temple stood, there is now an esplanade with various buildings, among them the Great Mosque and the Dome of the Rock. It is believed that the prophet Mohammed ascended into heaven from this Dome when he died, so it is the third holiest site of Islam. Some Jewish people think it is an aberration that this dome is there, because it is the site of their Holy Temple and the Holy of Holies.

I get out of the esplanade and into the Old City and I try to find an entrance to the mosque. Instead I end up in Via Dolorosa again, in front of St. Stephen's Gate (or Lions Gate), next to the Mount of Olives. As that was the next tourist attraction in my itinerary today and I am beginning to feel tired, I decide to head there instead of continuing wandering looking for an entrance to the mosque.

There are various churches on this mountain. My map is good enough to tell me roughly where they are, but not good enough to tell me how to get to them. There is not a soul in sight to ask, so I just follow various paths, in the belief that they will take me to at least one of those churches. I end up in a Muslim cemetery first and then in a Jewish one. I find a small patch of shade and sit down to rest and contemplate the Old City of Jerusalem, or rather the part of the wall that I can see from here, and the roofs - and the Dome - that stick out from behind the wall. From here, it does look like a city on the top of a mountain, as majestic as described in the sacred books. Fig 4

Looking at Jerusalem from this quiet position, I reflect on all this "Palestinian problem", and it seems to me that it is all summarised in that mosque built over there, on that soil that for the Jewish religion is holy soil, that has been invaded by this other religion that has planted its mosque there. For Zionist Jews, what needs to be done is dismantle that mosque and allow them to build a temple where the "Holy of Holies" should be, in the same spot where the Ark of the Covenant was kept one day. But this place is holy for the Muslims too because Mohammed ascended into Heaven from the Rock, which is also the Rock from which the rest of the world was made, therefore the Jews should build their temple elsewhere, if they want, or else continue lamenting at the other side of their invented West Wall.

The solution in other epochs would have been to simply expel entire populations from whole countries, forbid their entrance and destroy their holy places. But it is not possible to do that now without some one, somewhere, condemning it publicly.

Maybe the Israeli Government is trying to clean the country of Muslim people to later say that the mosque was left unattended so there was no point in keeping it standing. Maybe a hypothetical Muslim government would want to do just that with the Jews. The idea that seems the most common even among "moderate" Jews is that, yes, the Arabs have been here for hundreds of years, "but we were here first".

I will visit holy sites in trips for the rest of the week and then I will travel to Ramallah on Saturday.

Fig 4: View of the Old City of Jerusalem

First Saturday - **Jerusalem to Ramallah**

According to international treaties, West Jerusalem is in Israel and East Jerusalem is in Palestine. In reality, there is no border between West and East Jerusalem for Israeli citizens. For Palestinians it is altogether different. Most of them have no citizenship whatsoever. They may have a Palestinian passport but if they want to use it to travel to Israel or abroad, they need special permission from the Israeli authorities, and these may grant it or not, arbitrarily. They also have to ask for a special permit to travel to East Jerusalem, the part of Jerusalem that the international community in their treaties granted to a future State of Palestine. When the Israeli authorities give this permission, it needs to be renewed periodically if the Palestinian person in question wants to travel to Jerusalem again after the permission expires. So it is a commonly accepted knowledge among Palestinians and Israelis that the whole of Jerusalem is in Israel, not Palestine. This is contrary to UN resolutions and further agreements, but the rules and the practice imposed by Israel have established as much.

To most Palestinian people, permission to go to Jerusalem is simply never granted. Since some of the people who will give us a talk about Palestine belong to this group, international visitors who want to attend this talk need to leave Jerusalem for it.

I join a group of such internationals and we take a bus-taxi that will take us to Ramallah. The trip would normally take less than an hour in one of these taxis, but there is a checkpoint roughly in the middle of the journey and that will delay it for at least an hour.

The taxi-bus is like the one I took at the airport, only it had an Israeli number plate and this one has a Palestinian one. The Palestinian number plates have black characters on a white background or white ones on a green background. Latin numbers occupy most of the plate, and on the right, there is a small space for a Latin "P" and also for an Arabic letter. Israeli number plates are almost identical to those of the European Union. They can only be told apart by looking closely. They have an Israeli flag instead of an EU flag on the left of the number, and in the place for the member State initial there is "IL". The rest is the same: black Latin numbers and letters on white background.

As we approach the checkpoint at Qalandia in the taxi, the Apartheid Wall runs parallel to the road. It really is horrible. The wall we can see from this taxi is "only" five or six meters high. In other parts, it can be as high as nine.

Still, the worse thing is the sensation of destruction around it. It looks as if the road we are travelling on is still being built. I am told that in fact they are "destroying" it. After about five minutes of seeing rubbish and rubble on one side of the road and the wall on the other, the road goes away from the wall. As we continue travelling, on our left, in the other direction, I see a kind of police control where each car is stopped for two or three seconds and then let go. Those cars seem to have been allowed to go through this checkpoint. They seem newer and cleaner than this taxi or any other Palestinian vehicle I have seen so far. Someone points out that all of those cars that are allowed to go through have Israeli number plates. There is no vehicle with a "P" on the number plate allowed through the checkpoint.

I get the explanation that people with an Israeli "pass" can go through the control with no problem, but people without that pass - especially Palestinians, but also foreigners and anyone without that special pass - can not pass through this control by car. Palestinian cars are not allowed to pass through Qalandia. There is only one way for a Palestinian to get through the checkpoint: get in a taxi, leave it at one end of the checkpoint, then walk, and then get another taxi at the other end.

So our taxi driver stops before the checkpoint for pedestrians and announces that this is the last stop. We gather our belongings and start walking, first on the road, among the other taxis that have had to stop and let their passengers go, then on a muddy path. To my left, while I walk on the mud, there is the perfectly paved road that no one can use except Israeli cars. To my right, next to me, there is a high fence. At the other side of the fence there is another perfectly paved road with modern buildings and car parks, patrolled by armed soldiers that look at us with indifference, while we struggle in the mud, trying to step on hard soil and not get our feet too buried in the mud as we walk.

There are also soldiers on this side of the fence. They are actually everywhere. I look around me and one soldier grabs my attention. He is pushing a Palestinian-looking boy against the fence, beating him. Just like when I spotted the boy with the strange machine gun near Damascus Gate, time seems to have stopped and my heart is paralysed, while my legs go on walking without me commanding them. But my eyes are fixed on the soldier and the boy. When the soldier stops beating the boy he just walks away. My eyes are still fixed on the boy. He does not seem wounded, he just looks around and does not say anything, does not complain. I continue walking and finally look around too. No one else seems to have noticed the incident.

We arrive at some revolving gates made of iron bars. There is only space for one person and a rucksack at a time. Anything else needs to be thrown over the gate and then gathered from the ground on the other site. We are lucky we are travelling together and can catch each other's bags. I wonder what people do when they need to carry large things, when they need to move house... Carrying furniture or fragile stuff in these conditions is just out of the question.

We arrive at a small esplanade where there are a lot of taxis waiting for people who have gone through the checkpoint. So, we have gone through. We have not been checked, nor has our luggage been searched. I guess whatever goes into Palestinian territory is none of the soldiers' business, and the sole purpose of the whole checkpoint exercise is to delay every single person's journey by at least an hour, unless of course a soldier starts to beat you.

All the taxi men call us to attract our attention. I get conscious that what attracts them is not our pretty faces, but our foreign looks. A foreigner for them means lots of money. As one of my companions puts it, we are "walking money" for them.

Within days I will help with the olive harvest. Every one says that it is very nice, for the activity in itself and because the mere international presence makes it possible for families to harvest their olives, because without this presence the pressure and harassment from the military and the settlers make the task impossible.

First Sunday - **The three legal systems**

I get to an information session on the situation in Palestine and this is what I feel is worth highlighting here.

There are three legal systems, completely separated: the civil system, the military system and the Ministry of Interior.

The civil system is for Israelis, including "Arab-Israelis", but the Palestinians prefer not to use this term. They say Arab Israelis are simply Palestinians with a nationality and rights under the Israeli State. The rest of the Palestinians, including the Samaritans, are simply Palestinians, without rights.

Being an Israeli citizen means having rights. If an Israeli citizen is arrested, they need to be charged within 24 hours or else set free. In that sense it is similar to a western democratic system. The arrested person has rights, like a phone call, a lawyer... They can only be held for twenty-four hours without a judge's warrant. With a warrant, the maximum is thirty days. This is the civil system.

The military system is for the Palestinians. The accused Palestinian person can be held for up to eight days without a judge's warrant and we are told there is a projected change in the "law" in order to make it fifty days. With a warrant, there is no maximum of days s/he can be held without seeing a judge or a lawyer. We are also told that this warrant to hold a Palestinian arrestee for more than eight days and without a limit is given as a matter of routine.

There are hearings in front of judges in the three legal systems. In the civil system the hearings work similarly to what we know about hearings in Western Europe. In the military system, the hearings are just the bureaucratic and routine step to produce the warrant to keep a Palestinian detained, and this is usually automatic.

The third legal system is for foreigners. It was not created to deal with international "human rights observers", like us, but for the illegal workers from neighbouring countries. This is another story that is also interesting. When the occupation began, the Palestinians were given "permits" that proved they were allowed to work in Israel: that is, where they had always worked, but it was now Israeli territory.

Then at a certain point, all these permits were cancelled. Hundreds of thousands of Palestinians were left out of work. The economy that existed in Palestine before 1967 was completely destroyed by Israel, as most Palestinians were no longer allowed to work in Israeli factories, where they had had to go to work after Israel had forcibly expropriated their lands. And this included Gaza, the most densely populated territory in the world.

To replace all these Palestinian workers, foreign workers from neighbouring countries were allowed to come and work for very low wages. So low, they were better off working without a contract and becoming illegal workers, but receiving a more dignified salary. So a new legal framework was created to deal with deportations, etc., and it is this system that applies to us internationals. We can appeal to the civil system, but in reality what the appeal is about is not the deportation itself, but its terms.

Palestinians tried in the military system can also appeal to the civil system. However, there is not much hope in a system where the only people who can become judges are Zionist Jews - those who believe that every Jew has the right to return to Israel even if that means displacing anyone already living there previously.

In the civil system, for the Israelis, in order to jail someone it has to be proven that s/he is guilty. The accused person can only be detained for a maximum of twenty-four hours before being put in front of a judge, although the judge can extend this to up to thirty days. Then the prosecution has to prove s/he's guilty, like in western systems.

In the military system, for Palestinians, it is the defence that has to prove that the accused is innocent. Then the prosecution routinely alleges that letting the defence know the charges would mean to disclose "Secrets of State", so many Palestinians never get to know what they are accused of. The "task" is to "demonstrate" that the arrested Palestinian is "innocent" of "anything" that can be thought of.

Palestinians can be interrogated without a lawyer present, and without charges, for eight days, and once a warrant to extend this is asked for, there is no limit as to how long they can be interrogated. The judges are military as well and it is very rare that the warrant is not granted.

Some get detained for a crime that has not even been committed yet. When a Palestinian is accused of a feared crime that has not yet been committed "but which might be committed", the information that has led to the accusation is kept as secret information, on a secret file. The charges are secret, or are simply that they might do something that could compromise the security of the State. They can have a lawyer but the lawyer will not know the charges. And as for the place of detention, it is usually a tent in the desert.

These three systems have different laws, different tribunals and different police forces. There is the regular Israeli Police for the Israelis, the Army, and the Border Police. The regular Israeli police usually stay in the official territories of the Israeli State. The army and the border police are usually seen in Palestinian territories illegally occupied by Israel.

In the Palestinian occupied territories there is also the Palestinian police, but it has no real power. I am told that, on occasions, Palestinian police have been shot by the army - for them they are just armed Palestinians, and therefore terrorists - so you will never see any Palestinian police anywhere near checkpoints or military vehicles.

So in these Palestinian occupied territories, it is the Israeli Army and the Israeli Border Police that have the real policing power. The mission of the army is to defend the Israelis that live in occupied Palestine, the settlers. This has the following consequences: if a Palestinian throws stones at some settlers, the soldiers' duty is to defend the settlers, so they have the power to detain or even shoot the Palestinian. If it is the settlers that throw stones at, or shoot, a Palestinian, the soldiers' duty is still to defend the settlers. They have no power to arrest a settler even if they want to - or an international. At the most, they can detain them and call the border police so that they are arrested. What usually happens is that the settlers say that the Palestinian - or the international - attacked them first and they acted in self defence. Of course both soldiers and judges invariably believe the settlers. It is not rare that settlers attack, and even kill, Palestinians, and easily get away with it. Most times they are not even arrested.

Apart from the legal peculiarities, we are briefed about some cultural ones too. For example, when sitting with Palestinians, we must not show them the soles of our shoes. It is considered a very insulting gesture.

We are asked to respect their culture even if we do not understand it. We are also asked not to challenge the differences in treatment between men and women.

We women are asked to refrain from smoking in public and to wear long sleeves and long trousers - not long skirts, as we would look too much like Israeli settler women. We are told that if we wear revealing clothes, we will just notice looks and comments, but people will seriously complain to the Palestinians who work with us. Men are told that rules are a lot more relaxed for them, but are asked to smoke in private only and wear long sleeves and trousers too, in solidarity with us women.

We are also advised to always accept their hospitality, although sometimes it may seem a bit overwhelming for us. When we are staying with a family, we are never, ever, to bring food with us. It would be offensive to do that; it would be like telling them that their food is not good enough for us.

Some other facts that are interesting to highlight are:

- There are about seven hundred (700) military checkpoints on the roads in Palestine.

- Since the Gaza disengagement, flying checkpoints have increased about 300% according to the UN.

- For the Palestinians, the settlers are more dangerous than the soldiers. They often carry arms and they always have live ammunition, not rubber bullets or tear gas canisters like the soldiers. And the most dangerous settlers are the children, because they enjoy total immunity: whatever they do, they can not be arrested.

Bi'Lin

After this documenting session we are asked to go to a city where people are needed, Bi'Lin. In this city there is a demonstration against the wall every Friday. The wall has been declared illegal by the "international community". However, demonstrations against it are considered illegal, or at least the army does not consider them to be acceptable.

These demonstrations are usually attacked by settlers and soldiers, so internationals' presence is usually required so that the attacks are not so violent. We are told that settlers have the habit of smashing internationals' cameras and that if we complain they will say that we attacked them first, and we will no doubt be arrested. Apparently foreigners who have been arrested in Palestine are never allowed back again. So the advice is to keep away from them, avoid getting close to them so that they can not get close to our cameras, and be very careful when filming.

Now we learn that they have sent a letter where they say that the army will allow the demonstration as long as the Palestinians do not throw stones (I can not remember if there were any more conditions). The response has reportedly been that no permission has ever been asked for. The Palestinians, like the UN, think that the Israeli army should not be there in the first place, and therefore it should not be in a position where it could allow or forbid a demonstration.

What has apparently been happening lately is that the army has made incursions during the night, forcing their way into some homes and arresting mainly children, getting them out of their beds. The function of the internationals is then to get out, film and photograph these actions by the army. The internationals' presence does not stop the incursions or the arrests, but it usually ensures that they are at least not so violent.

So there we go, two girls and two boys, to spend the night in the company of various Israeli activists who also understand the madness of this occupation as it is. They tell us what is happening, we decide on who will do what in case we need to get out, and in case some one is arrested, and we go to sleep, hoping not to be necessary after all.

SECOND WEEK

Second Monday - **Nablus**

We did not need to go out to document anything. Very probably, we believe, they heard the rumour that some internationals would be there tonight too and they left it for another day.

We get up early and, after packing quickly, we set off to a city where help is needed to pick olives. It is a big group of us travelling to Nablus. We take a big coach service because, they say, we are much less likely to be stopped and questioned. In any case, we prepare a "story" in case we are stopped. It seems we can not say what we are really going to do in Nablus because helping Palestinian families is considered an act of terrorism.

It is not that they need cheap labour to do the harvesting. It is that those who have pieces of land near Israeli settlements suffer serious harassment from the settlers. Some farmers have been beaten up and they have also had their harvest stolen. Some have even had the donkeys they use to take the olives home stolen.

While in Nablus we will be staying in the neighbourhood of Balata, and, unless there are Israeli army incursions, we will be travelling daily wherever help is most needed with the harvesting. Balata itself is actually a refugee camp inside Palestine, full of people who were forcefully displaced from the lands they owned and on which their families had been living for centuries, to make space for the State of Israel to be created. This happened some years ago and Balata is now inhabited by the first refugees' children and grandchildren. They mainly lived off the produce of their lands before being displaced. Then they were forcibly dispossessed of them and forced to live in tents in camps like this. Now they are still living in the same refugee camp, only the United Nations have built houses for them. Due to the economic situation created by the Israeli state they can only live off international charity. The phrase "right to return" is used to refer to refugees like these. Some Israelis think these refugees' "right to return" is not even worth talking about; indeed some think that these people should no longer be called refugees because it was their parents and grandparents that were displaced, not them.

We join some more internationals in Balata and we are taken on a "tour" inside the refugee camp. Children stop us saying "Hello!" and "What's your name?" in English, probably not knowing exactly what they are saying, because we answer and repeat the question to them and they suddenly shut up. Old men smile or simply stare at us and some older kids shout out: "Welcome!".

We are told that there are actually various, maybe ten, refugee camps like Balata around Nablus. They house some of the hundreds of displaced refugees from the forties and seventies, Palestinian people that had been living from time immemorial in what later became internationally accepted Israeli territories, and who were massively displaced from all over Israel to make space for the Jewish returning from the Diaspora. They began living here in big marquees and tents and now they live in houses that are too small for the huge families. It is amazing how in these terrible circumstances people have continued to have hope and children. There are a lot of children per family too. The schools and the hospitals are run by some UN agency, but that is as far as the UN intervention will go.

The whole camp, which looks just like a poor village, is full of pictures of "martyrs", men and kids who have been killed by soldiers or died in jails, posted on walls or hanging from ropes fastened to two opposing windows. We are told that most families in this camp, if not all, have at least one member either in jail or killed by the Israeli army.

While in the middle of the "tour", we are invited to one of the houses for tea. The whole family is put to work to bring chairs around a tiny little table that will soon fill with glasses and tea.

There are a few pictures on the walls. The biggest one is a collage of portraits of men against a landscape that I am beginning to identify with Palestine: arid looking soil yet full of vegetation, even if only in parts. The second biggest picture is of the Dome of the Rock in Jerusalem.

Men and women, but mainly women, sit on the floor or on smaller chairs than those provided for us foreigners. A small boy with broken front teeth insists on bringing a glass of tea for each of us. The adults continue their conversation and our guide translates. He says that the men portrayed in the biggest picture are martyrs, men killed by the Israeli army, and one of them was from this family. He says this family has a few more martyrs, as well as this one.

The dead boy

He continues to explain something else but in the middle of the explanation he receives a phone call: there are some military movements up the northern mountains. There seem to be two injured men and another one missing. They need some internationals to look for these men on the mountain because if Palestinians alone go to the mountains to search, the army will simply shoot them. They know this from experience and the excuse the Israeli army has given in the past is that they thought they were terrorists, because of course only terrorists would go up a mountain after dusk.

Thus the visit, the tour and the storytelling stop abruptly. We all leave and get in taxis to the mountainous area where the movements have been reported. The taxis can not advance too quickly because the roads are pretty crowded, mostly with young men. Some of these look into the taxis, see some foreign faces inside, and those who speak English say "Welcome"; others just cheer. It feels like they know what we are here for, and gratitude just fills the air.

The taxis can only take us to the end of the road. The road ends where the Israeli army has put enough rocks on the road to block motor traffic. The army usually blocks roads in this way in order to "make movement more difficult for terrorists". In reality movement is made more difficult for all Palestinians, from those who are going to their jobs (those still lucky enough to keep one) to the emergency services, like ambulances.

We get out of the taxis and we learn that the two injured men have been taken to hospital, but there is still one missing man and he could be injured too. Our task is to find him.

We walk up the road past the road block and find only quietness, no movement, no vehicles, and no light other than moonlight. No one seems to be around. We continue up the mountain through a short cut, always up, up, and we keep calling the man's name, and shouting: "Internationals!" or "International medics!" to avoid being shot by Israeli soldiers.

We decide it is not a good idea to use torches that could attract soldiers' attention, as we are not sure if they are still around or not. It is already dark but the moon is bright enough.

We get back to the road and then up to yet another road block made of stones. We then decide to split in two groups; one will continue the way up following the path, and the other will go down the hill, where there is some vegetation where he could be hiding.

I join the group that goes up the hill and after a few minutes of walking, a Palestinian man joins us from the dark. He is the missing man's uncle, and tells us that, actually, the "man" we are looking for is a fourteen-year-old boy. He joins us in the search and after a turn in the path plus another hundred metres or so, one of the group sees someone lying on some stones at the side of the road and says:

"There he is."

A few men, including the boy's uncle, identify him and start shouting and crying and hugging him. Someone says:

"Check his pulse", but someone else replies:

"He is well dead".

The boy's uncle wants to carry him on his shoulders but a younger man stops him and lifts him. As he does so, the dead boy's head hangs lifelessly, still bleeding heavily. The young man takes him down the road from where we came and another one phones the other group to tell them to join us; the ambulances are already waiting there, at the point where they can not advance any more because of the road block.

The dead boy is handed to the medics and we are told to stay on this side of the roadblock. A western woman who now lives in Palestine tells us that, if we go with the boy's uncle, who is now with more members of the family, and they see us slightly distressed, they will forget about their own grief and put them-selves at our service with tea and food until they see us calmed down. Their sense of hospitality is so great, they will forget how distressed they are themselves. So we do not cross the roadblock until the family gets in one of the ambulances and leaves.

Some of us then go back to the mountain because we are told that there could be another man hiding in the area, maybe also injured. After about fifteen minutes we learn that yes, he is injured, and he is already in hospital. We then consider the search as finished and go back home.

When we get home, something unique happens. For the first and last time in this trip, I see a bunch of Palestinian men cooking food for us foreigners. This is how they are dealing with their pain.

Before starting to eat, one of the Palestinians speaks to us all:

"OK, what has happened is terrible, but this is our everyday life. He is now well and in peace, we remain here with our struggle. Unfortunately he is not the first one, he is number... a hundred and something..."

"A lot more than that."

"We wish he was the last one, but probably he will not be".

I am not too sure how many more nights I will go to sleep having these im-ages as the last thoughts of my day. The sequence of events repeats itself inside my head. The images I have are quite clear, considering it was night time. I can even remember people's faces. But then, from the moment I saw the body, these images become black and white in my brain.

Fig 5: Above, illegal civil settlement. Below, military barracks

Second Tuesday - **The Ottoman law**

Today we go to help out picking olives. The boy's whole family, probably the whole city, will bury the lifeless body we found yesterday, but if we go to the funeral instead of helping out in the fields, some other family will not be able to harvest their olives.

The Palestinian family we are helping today had permission to pick their olives yesterday but not today, so we are going with them in case soldiers or settlers turn up on their land; maybe we can reason with them. What is amazing is that we are talking about their own lands. If they do not have an official permission for each day that they want or need to enter their own land, soldiers or settlers can shoot and kill them, and they would not be found guilty because it would be considered that the land owners were "looking for it", for entering their own lands near an Israeli settlement without permission. Many families spend years without going to their own lands to avoid being shot. They only pick their olives when they have permission, which is not necessarily when the olives are ready to be harvested; permissions are not given automatically.

What the Israeli State is using quite a lot is an ancient law, from the time of the Ottoman Empire, according to which if some one does not visit their own land during a specific number of years, it is understood that they are not interested in it, and therefore anyone else can take possession of it. In other words: they threaten someone that they will kill them if they go to their own land, until they manage to get the land owner to never go there, and then they take possession of it with the excuse that they are not visiting it. This is what is being done in Palestine.

We get up early in the morning and at eight o'clock we get a taxi that takes us through roads and more roads, which are roads only by name, until there is no road to speak of, at the foot of a mountain. From there we continue up on foot. On top of the mountain we can see some houses and, a bit down the hill, a kind of barracks. The houses at the top are from the illegal civilian settlement, the thing under it is the army post. These settlements seem to be always built on mountain tops, so that they can control the Palestinian villages and lands within their line of sight, and with weapons and strong night lights. Fig 5

The olive picking is done by hand. They put some blankets on the ground surrounding the tree, and we all pick the olives one by one, throwing them onto the blanket. If the family have got the necessary resources, like this one seems to have, they put wooden ladders against the branches to pick off those at the top of the tree. Some also climb the trees without ladders, even the mother of this family climbs up, in her huge skirt and her sandals. Fig 6

Two or three hours after we start picking olives, the woman burns some small branches. She has already put some stones around the tiny little fire and a teapot on the stones. After a while she calls us to have a break and we find a proper meal there prepared for us: hot bread, tea, hummus, oil, yoghurt, zatah, olives...

about ten small dishes we all dip bread in. This is how they eat here, it seems. No one has an individual plate; we all dip the bread we have been given in these small dishes, one at a time.

We finish eating and go back to work. When there are lots of olives on the blanket, what we do is, we sit down on it and separate the olives from the leaves, and put the olives only in white sacks with a capacity for about fifty kilograms. Later these sacks will go on the back of the family donkey, which is patiently waiting a few metres from the last olives that we expect to work on. We "do" another ten olive trees and we have another break, again with some food.

We can not see the illegal settlement on the top of the mountain where we are working, but we can hear voices from time to time. At a certain moment, towards the end of the day, the father, from the top of a tree, sees some men coming towards his field. We ask him what he wants to do. He has a moment of hesitation. He has no permission to be here, in his grove. He has spent a whole day working on his field, and the fruit of it is still in the sacks, on the ground. If those men are settlers, they can rob him of the whole day's work, or the donkey, or the ladders, or all of it, and he will have no right to complain. Moreover, someone can get hurt. The priority of the Palestinian people that we help is always the security of the internationals who are helping them. And then their own, in second place.

Finally he tells us that he prefers to leave. We help them gather everything quickly, he puts the sacks on the donkey and we all go down the hill to their village. We then go on our way up to a place where a taxi can pick us up, at the beginning of the road.

Fig 6: Olive picking

Luckily, this man has not lost more than ten minutes of work. It is possible that the settlers have not seen us, or that they were just some security guards going on a round, and that they did not want to rob anything or even harass them, or that they did but thought better of it because of the presence of foreigners, but it is too risky to try to find out in such a vulnerable situation. We will come back here again tomorrow.

We get in our taxi and we pass through the village. Old men sit in front of their houses, some walk. They all have "kheffiyehs" on their heads. They all wear them white with stripes and squares of different colours; I learn that the colours have their political meaning. The black is worn by supporters of "Fatah", which I guess is a political party. The red is worn by supporters of PLFP (Popular Front for the Liberation of Palestine), and the green by supporters of Hamas.

Second Wednesday - **Oasis of peace**

Today we come back to the place where we were yesterday. We learn that this family lives from the produce of their trees alone; they do not have any other source of income. We ask them about the price of the olives. Last year the price per kilo paid to the farmers was 10 NIS, (New Israeli Shekels), about US$2.20. Some farmers were better off just saving the olives and using the oil, because with that price they would have lost money on the transaction. Like all producers of raw materials, they are at the mercy of the fluctuations in the international markets. They can sell very little to Israel, we are told, because the Israeli State is blocking the entry of Palestinian products into Israel; it is yet another way to squeeze them further. And they also need permission from the Israeli authorities in order to sell to other countries.

More people have come with the family to help out today and the task is a lot faster. They do not want to risk having to come back again without a permit to visit their own land, so, whatever we do not pick up today, will have to stay un-picked.

The bulk of the conversations are in English and mostly among the internationals only. Some Palestinian men can speak a bit of English. I suspect the Palestinian women can speak English too, but they do not really speak with us. Apparently the correct thing to do when you speak to a couple is to speak to the man only.

There is no problem with settlers or soldiers in the whole day and we leave at about four o'clock. We all agree that this business of olive picking is like an oasis of peace in the desert of war, at least for our eyes, because here on the mountain the feeling is very nice and peaceful, while the reality of the situation is all about oppression and silent and low intensity war.

We come back to the refugee camp of Balata, which looks like any poor neighbourhood of any city. People can already recognise our faces and we can also recognise some of the kids shouting and following us, saying "hello!" and "what's your name!". Sometimes they say "shalom", which is the greeting in Hebrew. We are told that the Jew is the only foreigner these children have seen, or recognised, so they assume that every foreigner is a Jew.

In the internet café from where I send these tales the manager asks us what we are doing here and we explain. He then gives us a special price, in solidarity.

Second Thursday - **Five years later**

We go to a different place to pick olives today. We are joined in the taxi by a few journalists. One of them speaks Arabic. When we arrive at a little village, a Palestinian man gets in the taxi and gives instructions to the driver. The taxi driver sets off, goes around the village and then stops and asks us to get out. We all get out and we follow the Palestinian, thinking that he will take us directly to the grove where we are to pick olives. But we rather seem to be wandering around the mountain without a route. To make things worse, we have to wait for the journalists, who are more interested in taking pictures than in walking. The Palestinian makes a few phone calls on his mobile and receives as many, all in Arabic. I comment to my colleagues how curious it is that there is such good coverage here in the mountains, while in the village it is a lot worse. Their answer is that it is not surprising at all, since we are near an illegal Israeli settlement. Everything possible is done to ensure that the settlers have a pleasant life and good mobile phone coverage is one of those things.

When the photographer who can speak Arabic catches up with us, we ask him to translate what the Palestinian is saying on the phone. He explains that he is talking to an Israeli activist who, from Jerusalem, is trying to get permission for our Palestinian man and his family to go and pick their olives. While he talks, the last journalist who had stayed behind arrives saying that there is a family that would like us to help them pick olives, and that we should all go there quickly, because all we are doing with this guy is wasting time waiting. We decide to go and help other families, only while the Israeli activist gets the permit for the family that in principle we came to help out.

We divide our group in two and each goes to a nearby grove to help with whatever the families are doing. These do not seem to need a permit - their land is far away from the illegal settlement.

The family I end up with seems quite well organised. The men climb the trees to reach the highest branches and the women stand on the ground to pick the olives that are lower down in the trees. When they finish off with each tree, the women move the blankets and take the olives to the centre of the grove, where another two women are sitting down sorting out the olives from the branches. They tell us by signs where we can help and after a while they call us to eat with them.

We all sit in a circle, but the plates are not in the centre of the circle for everyone; they are all next to us foreigners instead, and as the meal goes on, the plates come closer and closer to us, with the whole family encouraging us to eat more. I note that, as a result, the women sitting at the opposite end from us are hardly eating anything, but the other internationals tell me that it is best not to think about it because that is what they are like, this is how their hospitality goes and if we do not accept it they are going to feel offended.

Shortly after finishing the meal the Palestinian we met at the beginning of the day calls us and we all join again. He tells us that the Israeli activist has got the permission and he guides us up the mountain, to his land. As we go up, other men from his family join us; they do not allow their women to come with them because they are risking their own lives coming to this piece of their land, so close to Israelis, and they do not want to risk those of their women too.

We climb higher up the mountain and we find a foetid river with brownish, almost black water. Signalling the barracks we had assumed were military, they explain that it is a factory built a few years ago, that is discharging these waters that are damaging the land. Indeed, they prefer not to pick olives from trees that stand too close to the water.

This family's situation is the most precarious we have seen so far. They have hardly any blankets, and they have neither ladders nor a donkey. We have to put the olives directly into the sacks, as they are, with branches and all, and they are all obviously very nervous and in a hurry, eager to finish. It is also obvious that they have not come round here for a long time, because it is all covered with bushes and thorns that make walking quite difficult, and the olive trees are full of dry, useless branches that get badly in the way when trying to climb to get the highest olives. We have to pick up the olives in quite precarious conditions: I put them in my t-shirt as if it was an apron, another one puts them into the shirt pockets, the most fortunate ones have a plastic bag with them...

Three women join us after an hour or so. It looks like they have called them once they have seen that there are no soldiers or settlers around. A sixty-five year old man comes too, to give us his moral support and even an interview to whoever asks him for one. He allows us to photograph him and he tells us his story: his grandfather bought this land in the time of the Ottoman Empire. When he was five years old he inherited it and now it is his sons that have the responsibility over it, although their task is more and more difficult. No one of the family has been able to enter this land in the last five years. The result is wilderness, weeds and parasites everywhere, even in the trees. We have already seen that. Some of them even look more like bushes than trees. We also notice that someone must have come to steal olives, because many trees have hardly any olives in the parts easily accessible from the ground, and yet they are full towards the top. The only ones that can enter this land freely are the Israeli soldiers and settlers, from the top of the hill. There are also many trees burnt off. He tell us that this is a usual tactic of the settlers.

He also tells us that the putrid water has already killed many trees, and is now drying others off. And that in the year 2000 the settlers stole all they had harvested, their whole harvest, after all the effort to gather it.

We continue picking olives and I begin to feel like I am cheap labour for these people, because, so far, picking olives for them is all we have done, and we have not seen any settler or soldier yet. On this occasion, we have even waited for the permit in order to avoid a tense situation - I thought we were here to help deal with tense situations, not accompanying once the situation has been sorted. I get the answer that, had it not been for our presence here today, this permit would have never arrived.

At about two o'clock in the afternoon the journalists begin to say goodbye to everyone and the Palestinians misunderstand that it is all of us leaving. They all look at each other in panic and they beg us, they supplicate us not to leave yet:

"Please stay just one more hour, ok, just half an hour". Desperation shows on their faces. We explain that it is only two people leaving and the rest are staying and they calm down, and we go on frantically picking olives, between bushes, bending branches in order to reach the higher ones, getting scratched by the dried branches that no one can prune, passing over bushes, thorns and uprooted burnt trees.

Indeed one hour later the task is considered finished and we climb down towards the path quickly. Someone has brought a donkey and they load it with the olives; there will be scarcely fifty kilograms. The grandfather gets on the donkey too and a young man talks with us as we walk. He speaks English well because he is studying English Literature at university. He tells us that he is the fourth of six children, two of them girls, one of whom is also at University, reading Business Studies. When we go past their house he insists that we enter and eat something and chat. We refuse but they all insist again, so there is no choice.

We go into this humble but comfortable house. The women bring soap for us and when we have washed our hands we sit down in the living room with three of the boys. From my sofa I can see the two sisters, who have uncovered their heads now. One of them sits with us for a moment, then she leaves and an elder woman, surely the mother, comes in, bringing some bread that she has just made for us now. Then more people bring us tea, then a soft drink, then fruit juice, then more food... In the meantime we call the taxi driver who brought us here this morning and when the taxi arrives we say goodbye and leave.

As we arrive at our street in Balata we hear some shots in the distance. We do not hear screams though, so we figure that it can be some kind of celebration. We start going home but as we walk away from the main street we hear some music too. We turn back and we see the whole parade. First goes the music band, then more men and then some kind of plain clothes soldiers, all with weapons, some with a handkerchief around their foreheads, in a Rambo fashion. But their muscles are not so big; they are all almost children really, almost the same as the Israeli soldiers, who are rarely older than eighteen or nineteen.

A small procession follows the soldiers. We follow them and we arrive at a square surrounded by a fence. We stay outside the fence as spectators, trying to understand what is going on. The people who came in the procession have already sat down on white plastic chairs. There must be between six and seven hundred people. Most are men, except for about fifty or sixty women, all standing together on some lateral terraces. The music ends and various men talk, or rather shout, into some microphones, from a podium. The guys with the machine guns shoot into the air from time to time.

Another spectator talks to us in English and we ask him what they are saying. He answers that they are saying things like, they should go to the settlements and throw all the settlers out, things like that.

I do not quite know what conclusion to draw from what I have just seen and heard. On the one hand, it is a very macho-man show, with their handkerchiefs around their heads, their machine guns... on the other hand, all these people have grown up in a refugee camp, probably since the time when it was still a tent site, without water, without food... and they know they are not in this situation by chance, they know there is a very specific reason. For them, there was a "before" and an "after". Before they had dignified lives in their own lands, then they were thrown out of them into a temporary refugee camp made of marquees which was later made permanent. These guys and their families live in very precarious conditions in very cold, provisional houses, without hot water, without heating, with drainpipes that leave much to be desired and streets with neither pavements nor asphalt, just one surface of soil shared by vehicles and people that gets muddy with water that seems to come out of just about everywhere. At least we will eventually leave sooner or later. We can even go to Jerusalem from time to time to have a rest and a good shower and then return again. But these people have nowhere else to go. They stay here day after day, some going to school or university, knowing that there will be no job for them when they finish.

I guess the guys with the machine guns, and those who follow them, just want to end this situation and go back to some kind of dignified life, but they can not see any other way of achieving that than becoming "fighters".

Fig 7: Trench blocking Palestinian "road" to make it unusable

Second Friday - **Friendly settler with machine gun**

We go to a place that is much harder to reach today. Besides, only four of us in-ternationals are staying in Balata now, because today's demonstration in Bi'Lin needs to be supported and they have all gone there. Of those four, two are finish-ing their stay in the country today and they are going back home to their own countries, and the rest need a break. We are considering going back to Jerusalem, because in this flat we are asked not to have showers, as the water pipes are so bad. We have had soil stuck to our clothes and our clothes have been stuck to our skin for a few days now; it has been boiling hot every day and it seems like a good idea to go back to Jerusalem to have a good shower, a good rest and a good drink. But we can not do that yet.

Two new guys, D. and S., come today to stay for a few days. They arrive just in time to catch the eight o'clock taxi with us for today's "mission". We are told we have two options: either take just one taxi and go through the checkpoint, which will delay us for two hours minimum, maybe four, or take one taxi and then walk for about an hour to avoid the checkpoint, then take another taxi. Palestinians do not have this second option. We choose to use our privilege as foreigners to arrive earlier to help whoever needs us today. D. and S. will sleep there tonight so they take their rucksacks with them.

The reason why this journey takes hours is not the distance. In fact the place where we are going must be about twenty minutes away by car. But there is a military checkpoint on that road, and it seems that the traffic jam it produces delays the journey for about four hours, if not more. There is also an asphalted road - Palestinian roads in general are made of soil and dust - and it has no check-points, but it is for Israeli settlers and soldiers only.

On previous days the taxi has taken us up to a point where the road turns into a rocky path and it can only be used on foot. Today the road does not seem to fin-ish at the spot where the driver stops; it seems to go on. We say goodbye to the taxi driver and continue walking on the road until we end up in an open field.

Once there, we are in full view of an Israeli settlement on the top of the hill, which is of course next to an army barrack. This is why the taxi driver stopped back at the edge of the village earlier: if he gets in view of the settlement, he and his taxi are in danger of being shot - the excuse being, a Palestinian (therefore a potential terrorist) being "too close" to some Israeli population. As for ourselves, our foreign appearance seems to be enough to grant us the privilege to walk on this open field without being shot at. We walk a few meters and we see that the road is cut short, this time by a trench like those used in the war. It must be at least a kilometre long. Fig 7

The bottom of the trench is full of rubbish and debris. We go down into the trench in order to cross it, get through all the rubbish as best we can and then up on the other side of the trench; then we go on walking. What is left of the road goes through fields with no trees, except one grove where there are small olive trees. They look like newly planted trees.

The soil is very stony, like other soils we have picked olives on. We cross a perfectly asphalted road - one of those for exclusive Israeli use - and when we reach the next road, this time dusty and without asphalt, we find that a taxi van is waiting for us. We have avoided the checkpoint that would have delayed us for hours.

This second taxi drops us off at the door of a public building that could be the town hall or a school. There are posters on the walls that explain graphically how to vote. We are invited into an office and more and more men come in and talk in Arabic. We are offered to sit on a sofa and some men sit on chairs. The conversation grows louder and louder and suddenly they all stop talking. One of them tells us in English that he is the Mayor, and asks us where we are from.

"From the USA", one responds. The mayor smiles and says in a basic English:

"With the people from America... very good, but with Bush..." and he makes a funny face, and we all smile. He asks the same question to a few of us and he shows that he knows the names of the presidents of all the countries we come from.

After a few minutes of waiting, another man turns up at the door and we all get up: this is the farmer we are to help out today. He will take us up the mountain to wherever he can manage with an old all-terrain vehicle, and from there, we will continue on foot.

Once up on the mountain, as we walk, we see an army vehicle parked on the road at the bottom of the hill. A uniformed soldier is next to it with his big weapon. He calls after us as loudly as he can. The Palestinian answers, in English, that we have permission to pick olives for three days. It seems that this is a good enough answer for now and we start picking olives, but after a few minutes he calls us again and we realise that there are two soldiers climbing the hill towards us, with their weapons and all. D. and S. climb down to tell them that we do have a permit. They make them wait near their vehicle while they make a few phone calls to check whether we are telling the truth.

When the soldiers are satisfied, D. and S. come back with us and we go on working, advancing towards the most "dangerous" part of the grove, next to a fence. As we approach it, we realise that this fence separates Palestinian land from the land that now belongs to the illegal Israeli settlement that sits on the top of the hill, about eight hundred metres from where we stand. Within that space, there are two other fences separating both zones - three fences in total to protect the illegal Israeli settlement from the legitimate Palestinian owners of the land.

Sometimes the protective fences have electronic sensors. We think this is the case this time because ten minutes after climbing the tree closest to the fence an army jeep comes up the path on the other side of the fence. It goes up and down a few metres various times and then it leaves. Five minutes later the army jeep comes back, this time followed by another jeep, this one white. Several men come out of the vehicles, some in military uniforms, others in plain clothes, all with machine guns.

One of those in plain clothes tells one of us to go over to them. She hesitates - the rule is not to speak to the settlers when we are with Palestinians who may not speak English because they do not know what we may be telling them; all they can see is a friendly conversation with the very people that steal their olives, beat them up and kill them with impunity. But the man in plain clothes has a weapon and repeats his order, so my comrade walks towards him. He asks her:

"Where are you from?"

She hesitates again, but decides that saying the name of the country she comes from will not do any harm, so she says it.

"And what is your name?"

This time she is not having it. The man then says he is coming in a friendly way and that he wants to offer her biscuits. She refuses politely and he says, laughing, that they are not poisoned.

A pretty silly conversation follows about how ignorant we are because, as we just pick olives, we can only see one side of the coin, "... which, by the way, it does have two sides, you know?" And that we do not understand that the Jews need to defend themselves from the Palestinian terrorists, because the Jewish, at the end of the day, are only good people who have every right to this land because they have been living up there, in the settlement, for no less than twenty years.

D. goes to speak with the Palestinian couple we are helping. They have walked away from the fence long ago, with fear showing in their faces. The Palestinian man can only manage to say:

"You, here" - and we understand that he wants us to walk away from the armed men and join him. We leave the tree where we are with regret because it is truly full of olives - although it is pretty impossible to climb to the highest branches due to the lack of pruning during the years they could not come, probably because of harassments like today's. Who knows what this settler would have done if the ones climbing the trees had been Palestinians instead of foreigners from rich countries.

The settler's sons

We start to gather our backpacks to leave, making sure that no bag is left behind. Suddenly a bunch of settler children appear next to the cars. With very aggressive faces, they start to scream at us:

"I'm gonna kick your ass!"

"Aaaahhh ha haha ha, you are all leaving now, you have to leave, we've won, you're gone!"

As I walk away, the last thing I hear, just before they throw the first stone at us, is:

"I hope you die!!"

The friend who wanted a friendly conversation is nowhere to be seen, and neither are the soldiers. The children continue to throw big stones at us, reaching pretty long distances. I take out my camera and they start moving, getting out of my field of vision, hiding behind trees that stand between them and me. It shows they are very experienced in hiding from cameras. While we finally walk away from the fence, we can still hear the children laughing, and the stones are still raining towards us, but we are no longer within their reach.

A few women and a few more men join us as we walk back down the hill, one of them on a donkey. It looks like they have been waiting for us the whole time, expectant and too afraid to climb up themselves. They put various sacks full of olives on the donkey and a boy rides it away. Then we come up to a parked van and the men put the rest of the sacks, almost empty, into it, and they invite us to get in. They give us refreshments in cans of a well-known multinational brand and I can only notice in private the absurdity of supporting a brand that behaves the way this one does while we are doing what we are doing.

We are taken to the town hall or school where we were at the beginning and more men and some elderly people join us. They shake hands with all of us and the one who speaks English tells us that they want us to eat with them and their families. When I am already accepting - as refusing would be almost offensive in most cases - we remember that it has taken us two hours to get here, and if we are lucky it will take us another two to get back. If we start to accept an invitation now, and given the concept of time that these people have, it can get dark before we start walking back, and walking back the same way we came, in the dark, in full view of armed soldiers that could mistake us for Palestinians, is definitely not a good idea. Besides, D. and S. are staying in this town tonight and they can accept the invitation for us. So we say goodbye to them and they get us a taxi.

The taxi comes loaded with more people from Balata who are travelling back there too. We settle ourselves in the taxi, guessing that this time we will have to use the length of the road, going through the checkpoint that can take between two and four hours of waiting in the queue.

At a certain point in the middle of the journey, one of the passengers gives some money to the driver and tells him to stop. The taxi driver stops. The man tells us that it is better for us to get off here and he opens the door for us. We get out of the taxi and I realise that we are in the very same place where the last taxi picked us up before, so we only have to go back the same way we came this morning.

So this is what has happened: this man, who looks more humble than us, has paid our fare and has put us in a safe place so that we can go on without going through the roughness of the checkpoint, giving us the very privilege he can not afford himself. If the Palestinians dared walk across the fields to avoid the checkpoint, the soldiers would shoot at them from the outpost, on the mountain top. But we are foreigners and white.

So there they go, to the checkpoint, where they will be held for, who knows, two, three hours ... while they wait to be allowed to pass - if they are allowed at all. I look at the man full of wordless gratitude. He looks back at me with a smile. We all say goodbye with a last nod and, feeling a lump in my throat, I throw my bag on to my back and start to walk with my colleagues, back to Balata refugee camp where we are staying.

Second Saturday - "When I grow up I want to be a martyr"

There is no need for internationals today, it seems, so we take the day off and decide to go shopping in the main street to support the local economy. I am advised to buy soap, hand made with olive oil.

There have been children waiting at our door every day so far, shouting "what's your name" all the time. Most faces change from one day to the next, but the boy who served us tea on our first day is here every day, waiting for us to come out to the street to wish us a good morning in his own way.

Today the children are not waiting; we are going out of the house at mid morning so they should all be at school. But our constant friend is here today too, this time with a school bag on his back.

With our ultra basic Arabic we ask him why he is not in school. Knowing that we will not understand him if he speaks to us in Arabic, he uses basic English and gestures. First he says "school" making a face of disgust. Then he spits. Then he steps his foot strongly on the spit. Then he points at himself with his first finger and then, with the same finger, he points at the pictures of the dead fighters.

Back home, we tell this to M. He says:

"The boy's case is not an isolated one, but the Palestinian people, at the end of the day, are not that much different from any other people. Everyone wants to have a normal life, raise a family, go to work, come back from work, hug their children. We are not violent people. If the children want to be fighters, and if people blow themselves up killing other people, it does not come out from within us, that is not our way of being. It comes from desperation, from the occupation and the conditions of this occupation."

We respond to this with silence, as we did with the child before.

Y. comes to the flat to take us somewhere else this evening:

"Whoever wants to come and see my society, you can come now". Everyone gets ready to go with him. No one makes a comment, and the general silence makes me too afraid to ask. For this reason I assume that "my society" means some secret or clandestine society. So I just walk with the group, almost in complete silence, which reinforces my assumption. To my pleasant surprise, the "society" is something like a mainstream youth club where he and other committed people try to get the local youth out of the spiral of violence that ends up in a picture on a poster in the street.

He tells us about the activities that take place here, recreational and educational as I understand them. He also tells us the stories of some of the young people, "shebab" in Arabic, that have been kind of "his pupils". Some have gone on to university, some have stayed in the camp, some have been arrested, and a few others have been killed.

We go back to the flat and while we are cooking dinner E. comes to visit. She is very upset because she has heard the news about the boy we found dead. She has also learnt more things from the acquaintances of the victim and she is seeing the manipulation of the media and the Israeli authorities, for the umpteenth time.

It seems that the other two victims have said that they had gone to the mountain to explore a derelict building that they had seen one day. I remember seeing that building on the night we found the boy; it looked like a mosque. What the news bulletins are saying is that they were trying to plant a bomb. They have also changed the age of the victim, adding years, and the way in which he died. E. has been thinking about the way we found him: there was a lot of blood, and not only on his head, but also all over his trousers, although he was not bleeding from any of his legs. The army is saying that they did not shoot to kill. They always say that they shoot at the legs, but there is no shot on the head if you are aiming at the legs. Besides, the size of the wound on his head made it obvious that he was shot at point-blank range. They also say that the boy was running away, and that is why he fell down on the stones where we found him, at the side of the road.

Her conclusion is that the boy was executed in such a position that the blood fell on his trousers, so most probably he was on his knees when he was shot, and he bent over his stomach as he fell, and blood from his head fell on his trousers. And then they took him to where we found him to make it look like he was running away, which they did not quite manage because the body fell on its back. When you are running you do not fall on your back.

These are her conclusions. I personally think that they sound very logical and quite a lot sounder than the army's explanations, and I would be very surprised if, on the outside chance that the army or the media ever bothered to try to refute these allegations, their explanations could resist even the slightest bit of analysis. But, since it was just one Palestinian man from a refugee camp, his death is not even worth investigating.

Second Sunday - **Martyrs**

M. tells us that there is a huge respect in Palestine and other countries for "internationals" like us, who, M. says, leave "the comforts of your homes, your education, your work, your families, to come here and suffer with us Palestinians". And he goes on to thank me for supporting what sounds to me like the Palestinian "cause". I do not feel too comfortable with his assumption, so I answer:

"Look, it's not that I especially like Palestinian people. I am here because you are oppressed and your dignity is being taken away from you. But if it was the Palestinians doing that to the Israelis, I would do this for them."

He quickly replies:

"Of course, of course".

He also says that he feels a lot of respect for all the martyrs, but that he feels a very special respect for Rachel [Corrie, the girl from the USA who was killed while trying to stop the demolition of a Palestinian home by Israeli bulldozers] and Tom [Hurndall, the boy from the UK who was killed while he was trying to protect some small Palestinian girls]. M. looks away and I get the impression that he got to know both of them.

Y. calls us around mid morning to tell us there is a new martyr today, a man who was killed in the small hours of this morning. We gather our cameras and go to the house where all this happened, to document the result of the destruction.

We can still smell the smoke when we arrive. There are bullet holes and broken glass everywhere, a television set broken by a bullet, smashed lamps, windows that are no longer windows but mere holes in the wall... and other holes in internal walls caused by explosions. Y. explains what he knows and then lets the man of the house speak, as he can also speak English. We are informed that the man who has been killed did not actually live in this house, he was just visiting when the army came. So it looks like he had been followed.

Although it looks very much like the army was inside the flats destroying everything, we are told they were not: had they been, the telly, for instance, would not just have a bullet hole; it would have been lifted then smashed against the floor. All the destruction we see here has been made by bullets shot from the street.

The man tried to escape from one flat to another trying to avoid the bullets, and he finally went out to the garden. Once there, he was shot dead and then run over by a bulldozer, which also destroyed a wall in the garden.

The soldiers then ordered all the neighbours to get out of their flats. The neighbours, of course, complied, and, to make sure there was no one remaining in the flats, the soldiers opened fire against the walls and windows. That was probably when all this destruction happened.

Then they ordered everyone to take off their clothes. A neighbour tells us that they were left outside, in the cold night, completely naked, for about four hours.

This neighbour complains that this man, whatever he was guilty of, had nothing to do with them, he was visiting another family and they, just by the fact that they were neighbours of the visited family, were punished too. He asks us:

"Who are the victims?" - in reference to the official Israeli discourse according to which the Israelis are the victims of Palestinian attacks.

When the men finish their explanations I concentrate on the eyes of the women and children who follow us through the house in silence. Then I wander around the rooms on my own. More broken glass on the floor, more bullet holes in the walls and the ceilings. There is debris in rooms that were once comfortable, someone's home, a few hours ago. Whole windows have been destroyed and now they are only holes in the walls, leaving the rooms open to the street. An elderly woman is sitting on a bed, covering her face with her hands. She is sobbing. I leave her there, alone in her desperation, and I join my colleagues.

THIRD WEEK

Third Monday - **The wall, explained**

It is proposed that we go to Jayyous, a small village where internationals have been needed for some time now, and I volunteer. No one else volunteers so I agree to travel with A. and another colleague, since they say it is dangerous for a woman to travel alone. They are going somewhere near to where I am going. I ask them when they are setting off and they tell me they do not know. Then suddenly, at a given moment, with their bags on their backs already, they tell me:

"We are going now, are you coming?"

We get on a bus that we will have to leave before the checkpoint, because people are only allowed to go through it on foot. At the end of the checkpoint there are some revolving gates through which it is very difficult to pass certain sizes of luggage. As we do look quite like foreign tourists, we are not asked any questions and we are allowed to jump the queue, while some four hundred Palestinian people have been queuing for hours. At the end of the queue, a soldier opens a Palestinian's bag and gets everything out of it.

We arrive at the city where A. and his friend are going and there I join other people who are travelling to Jayyous too.

I also speak to P. about the subject of having to depend on our "fellow" men colleagues and she tells me that she, and other women she has spoken to, are also quite fed up of having to depend on the men. They have reached a point where they have decided to run risks and now they travel on their own. P. is quite happy with the treatment she receives from the Palestinians. She is not so happy about the treatment from the soldiers, but they are so racist, they hardly question you if you are not too dark.

I try to speak with Z. about this and the only answer I get is "I see what you are saying. But I like making my own decisions". The funniest thing is that this bloke has come here with a spirit of solidarity, and blah blah blah.

We go through another checkpoint and, once on the other side, we take a taxi and we wait for it to fill up. B. and Z. mumble something to each other and B. gets out of the taxi. Half a minute later B. comes back with two bananas and gives Z. one of them. I figure out then that when they were mumbling he was offering to buy Z. a banana too. I ask him if it would be too much of a hassle to buy me one and he answers: "It is going to be difficult". Indeed, the taxi is now full and sets off. I go without a banana while they placidly eat them without offering. It reminds me that I have gone for hours without eating and I begin to feel unwell.

When we arrive at the coach station we realise that we have half an hour until the coach we need sets off. I decide that I do not want to be that long with this pair of selfish guys and I venture into the surroundings. In the street next to the coach station there is a market with fruit and vegetables. There is a continuous and noisy activity but suddenly every one looks in the same direction, towards the end of the street, and they point to it and they speak loudly. I look in that direction and I see various military men with khaki clothes and of course machine guns, some of them walking quickly, some of them running. For a few seconds there is a total and expectant silence and we can only hear the noise the soldiers make. Then the soldiers disappear into distant streets and the market goes back to normality. I concentrate on the bananas and apples in front of me and ask the man who is selling them whether he speaks English, and another man responds. I ask him for a banana and he understands that I want a kilo. After various unsuccessful attempts, I grab a loose banana and I give it to him. Then I ask for two apples and the same happens. I actually would love to buy one or two kilos of each, but we are travelling and changing taxis and coaches at each checkpoint and in each city, and carrying our luggage on our laps or next to our seats if we are lucky, so I really can not get food even for the whole journey, only the food I am going to eat right now. I ask him how much it all is and he shakes his head and a hand: nothing. Excuse me? As if these people could afford to go about giving their merchandise away. I insist and he repeats that I should not pay. I am going to enjoy travelling on my own.

J. joins us in the next city. He tells us that a couple of nights ago the Israeli army made yet another incursion in the village where I spent my first night with a few others, Bi'Lin. For them, this time has been simply another raid to make arrests. The aim is to arrest Palestinian children that have taken part in demonstrations. It is interesting: the wall has been declared illegal by the international community - the same international community that created the Israeli State in the first place. Peaceful demonstrations are held against that wall that has been declared illegal and those demonstrations are declared illegal by the Israeli State, thus mocking the very international community that created and supports it. As the demonstrations go ahead anyway, the army force or kick open people's doors, in the middle of the night, when there are not so many internationals around. And they do it with impunity. And now I learn that, to prevent these people from claiming compensations for the damages caused by these incursions, they call them "war actions".

J. says that the presence of about twenty activists in the village two nights ago, between Israelis and internationals, should have made the soldiers think twice about it. Even so, sixteen boys from the village were taken away. Some

Palestinians came out of their houses to resist the detention and the invasion. After an hour of home invasions and arrests, the army left.

J. explains that there is a non-violent continuous campaign, lasting for some years now, against the "annexation barrier". The barrier can consist of a road, a wall, or a fence. In Bi'Lin it consists of a fence of three to six metres high, with barbed wire on the top and razor wire on the ground. The fence is either electrified or, preferably, electronically provided with sensors that will report any contact made with it, or any presence near it, to the nearest control tower. The order that the soldier in the control tower has, when there is any contact with this fence, is to shoot to kill.

In theory these barriers or fences have the function of providing the Israeli settlements with security against Palestinian terrorists, and by extension, all Palestinians. In reality, the Israeli government does not even bother to hide the fact that the settlements have the function of annexing more and more land to the Israeli state.

From what I have seen so far, the barriers and fences provide the triple functionality of separating the unarmed Palestinian population from the armed and mostly fanatical Israeli settlers, while providing the soldiers and settlers with excuses to shoot to kill; separating Palestinian villages from the lands they depend on for their survival; and annexing territories to the Israeli state. The general objective we perceive only after a few weeks here is to drive away the whole of the Palestinian population: ethnic cleansing.

J. says that the campaign against this barrier has the support of hundreds of Israeli and international activists and that this campaign has been violently opposed by the Israeli army. And Z. says that Israel has designed the route of this barrier in particular in order to annex sixty per cent of the cultivated land of this village and expand the local illegal Israeli settlement. All Israeli settlements in Palestinian territory have been declared illegal by at least one international institution: Palestine has been declared an occupation by the UN, even an illegal occupation, as apparently there are such things as legal occupations, and the Geneva Conventions prohibit the establishment of civil population settlements on occupied territories by the occupying force.

Jayyous

It is already dark when we arrive at the house of the land owner who has asked for international help, known as "Abu A.", which translates as "Father of A.". It is frequent for people to change their name when they have their first male child, to a name like "Father of.." and then the name of the first child.

Abu A. receives us with a copious dinner that we all needed, and we ask him what the situation here is like.

"You want to know what the situation is here? I will tell you what is the situation here, in a moment".

When we finish our dinner he takes us to the living room. There is a poster of Rachel Corrie stuck on the wall. Abu A. shows us pictures of bulldozers uprooting his centenary olive trees and maps of his land with the local annexation wall that isolates the village from its lands. He explains that most of the village's land is right on the other side of the wall that the Israeli State keeps building to annexe more and more extensions of Palestinian land illegally. All that land is now between the annexation barrier and the line that keeps being referred to as "The Green Line", established by the United Nations as the frontier between the current State of Israel and the future State of Palestine.

There are several gates, all numbered, along this fence, guarded by soldiers of the Israeli army. No inhabitant from the village can use the gate that stands on the shortest way to their land. The soldiers do not say the reason, but there are already excavation works preparing for the construction of new houses, expanding the Israeli settlement on the other side, which should not be there in the first place. This is what they uprooted Abu A.'s trees for, to expand the illegal Israeli settlement. Later they re-planted them in the Israeli settlement.

The fact is, up until a few years ago, Abu A. and other farmers did have permission to use this gate, although not with tractors, so people had to go back to using donkeys, thus forced to take a step backwards in rural development. Now they have to use the next gate down the fence, which means a twenty seven kilometres journey. Plus the twenty seven kilometres to come back once on the other side. On a donkey or on foot. An hour and a half journey to go round the fence instead of a few minutes walk through the gate right next to the illegal expansion of the illegal settlement. The result is that those who have to walk or ride that distance on their donkeys can hardly ever go to their own lands, because it is so difficult to get to them. Then there are the more fortunate cases. Abu A. has a tractor that is allowed to go through one of the gates, but he also has various sons, who are not allowed into his land at all. Formerly, he also had employees. But now, whoever wants to see to those lands from the Palestinian side needs special permission from the Israeli authority that is only conceded to those who can prove that they are the owners of the land and have never been arrested. This leaves out all the sons of Abu A. and all his employees. It also keeps him away from any political activity, like demonstrations, because they usually arrest "uncomfortable" people in them. If he is arrested just once, he will lose the permission to work on his land, and with it, the land itself, and then his still-non-existent-country will have lost part of the territory that the United Nations has "guaranteed" it, once it exists, because it will have been confiscated by the Israeli State "legally". This is the most comfortable way of confiscating land "legally": they arrest the proprietor, they revoke his permit to enter his land. In this context, the Israeli government is using a law created during the Ottoman Empire according to which if a land owner does not tend to his land for three years, then that land can be confiscated. The Israeli government interprets this as "becomes Israeli property". I guess this is where we internationals come into play; at least we turn up from time to time on these lands, using our privilege as Israelis or foreigners, helping out with the olive harvests, to at least delay the confiscation of their land using this law.

Abu A. has been talking to us for a few hours now. He stops for just a moment to let the information sink in and J. reflects on this, more or less with these words:

"So, only those who can prove that they own the land are allowed to enter the area that stands between the legal wall and the illegal wall, which are about six kilometres apart in this area. If one of these people is ever arrested then they will have no right to access their own land, no matter how many generations this land has belonged to your family for, or how much your own survival depends on the labour of the land. This access permit means that the farmers can not even hire workers to help them work on the land, which makes them become full time farmers and totally dependent on the produce of their harvest."

And now Abu A. tells us they are not allowed to sell their mandarins and other fruit in Israeli territory, or even in their own village. Which, now being completely dependent on the produce of their lands if they do not want the Israeli authorities to confiscate them, leaves them without any income. Some look for a job to survive this situation. Not an easy task where unemployment is about 60%, where the economy is completely squeezed by the occupying forces, and where those forces have not allowed the occupied population any freedom of movement to find work elsewhere for decades.

My own reflection is:

"In a normal country, if someone has his land confiscated by the State, it is a personal drama. But here, when the Israeli State confiscates land from a Palestinian in the territory under the occupation, that land becomes Israeli territory, that is, it goes to another country. Politicisation of private life. A private robbery made into a political robbery, and left unpunished."

Abu A. continues his simple speech: This has not been done in this area yet, amongst other reasons, because the local people have resisted against the theft of land for a long time. Abu A. has sold all his valuables, including his wife's jewellery, in order to try and stop the illegal confiscation of his lands. Right now, the work on the land where his trees were uprooted has stopped because Abu A. has proven, in Israeli courts, that this land is his and that the Israeli government has no right to expand the settlement on the land where his trees have been uprooted. However, just a few days ago, he saw some bulldozers working and heard explosions tearing off the soil and the rock to make excavation easier.

What usually happens is that the illegal Israeli settlement is built while the court proceedings are slowly taking place - it can be years. Then, when the sentence is pronounced, something called "facts on the ground" is alleged, which means something like: because the houses are already built and there are people already living inside them, and it would cost a lot to evict their occupiers and demolish them, as a lesser evil things stay as they are, and the legal process is effectively nullified. Apparently these "facts on the ground" are, or have been, supported by the USA government in international negotiations.

After this very long conversation, Abu A. takes us to the house where we will spend the night, with the family that we will help tomorrow.

This family offers us dinner too, while the sons and daughters watch a film from the United States with subtitles in Arabic on TV. The sitting room consists of a mattress - two more when we arrive - and a mat on the floor acting as a table. At once the place is filled with little plates full of food that the mother has made right there and then, and we all dip bread.

The father, F., and his nephew, H., speak to us in English, as well as another man, older, who introduces himself as F.'s uncle. His English is more basic than the others' and he is the only one who wears a kheffiyeh over his head. He tells me stories about his childhood, especially about the area of land his father used to own, and which the Israeli government has confiscated illegally. He also tells me that when he was a child he used to go to school with Abu A., but his parents could not afford to send him to university, and that is the reason why his English is not as good as Abu A.'s.

There are at least eight children in the house. It is difficult to count them because most of them are playing and moving around. It looks like there are only two rooms in the house so accommodating us is not the easiest task in the world. The boys will sleep with their father in the children's room and I will stay in the couple's room, with the mother and the youngest child.

They tell us where the toilet is and we use it, one by one. From later conversations I learn that we all, one by one, looked for the toilet seat, thinking that they were pulling our leg or that there had been a serious misunderstanding. After some time of disconcerted searching we all saw the hole in the floor, with a small platform, the size of a foot, on each side.

After using the toilet they explain to us that, although we can leave our batteries charging overnight, they will only be actually recharging for a few hours, because there is no electricity during the night.

I go to the parents' room and the mother offers me to sleep in the bed, where the youngest child is already sleeping, with the light on. I guess that if I accept she will sleep on the floor so I tell her I prefer to sleep on a mattress on the floor.

She insists and I have to refuse several times, but eventually she puts a mattress on the floor for me. I settle down between the blankets, still with the light on, and I wait for her to come to the room to sleep. Time goes by and she is not coming, so I get up and switch off the light to sleep. Right then the child wakes up and starts crying. I switch the light back on and shortly afterwards I fall asleep, with the light still on and, when I wake up at four in the morning, the light is off. There will be no electricity now until eight o'clock in the morning.

Third Tuesday - **Water rationing**

I wake up when it is still dark outside and too early to receive any electricity, so there is no light in the room. The mother of the family has got up and dressed; she is praying in whispers, standing up, next to her bed. When she finishes she opens the door and leaves. I also get up and put the blankets and the mattress in the corner where they came from.

We all get up at about half past six in the morning and go out without having breakfast, to get as much daylight as possible. Outside, the nephew we met yesterday, H., joins us.

We all get on the tractor trailer, including the mother and the youngest child. We then head to one of the gates that they now have to use to go to their land. On the way, still in the village, another family approaches the tractor and F. switches the engine off. F. speaks with the man and his wife speaks with the woman. Exactly the same as in any western village when two families meet.

As we arrive at the soldiers' sentry box I get my camera out to record the moment and both the mother and H. tell me "no" quickly, with their hands and heads.

While F. discusses with the soldiers about the reasons why we are not allowed to pass, a western woman with a waistcoat with the name EAPPI on it comes back from the gate. She has not been allowed to pass either. She sits down on a stone by the road and she looks at us and writes on a notepad while F. speaks to the soldier.

When we speak to her, after not being allowed through ourselves, she says that the permission-giving "system" (whatever unwritten "system" there is) is not consistent at all:

"I have been allowed to pass on other days. Just yesterday, for example, some other foreigners were allowed to pass. Every soldier is an official; they allow some people, they don't allow others... Just as they please. It's a completely arbitrary way."

She has been documenting all this, as it seems to be what EAPPI does at this particular gate. EAPPI stands for Ecumenical Accompaniment Programme in Palestine and Israel. She also tells us that there are two soldiers for each person in the settlement. This confirms to me that settlements have nothing at all to do with "getting both cultures together", that they are an outright military operation and that this gates business has nothing to do with security at all. Some are allowed, some are not, at random, with no criteria. It blatantly is just a matter of playing with people's time and resources, to make them so fed up and their lives so impossible that they have no other choice but to leave their lands.

All you can do when an armed soldier tells you that you are not going through the gate is to shut up and go back, so that is what we do. Worse than that is seeing F. speak amiably with the soldier and shake his hand. But he has to do it because he needs to maintain a bit of peace and good relations that will at least allow him to use this gate from time to time, next time the soldier in charge feels good enough about himself and F. to let him through.

F. is going to try to get to his land through another gate. That other gate is one of those where only land owners are allowed to pass, so we will need to try yet a different gate, a few more kilometres away. Abu A. and F. arrange for a car to take us so we do not have to walk for hours.

F. leaves us on a busy road and a car collects us ready to take us to the next gate, twenty five kilometres away, while the family gets through the one where only they have permission to pass as land owners.

At the next gate, where our driver was sure he would be allowed to pass with his car, we are not allowed to pass either, and we have to go all the way to the next one - a further fifteen minutes or so by car. Finally we get through to the Israeli side of the wall-fence on foot, and, bordering the Israeli settlement, we finally get to the land where we are going to help out with the harvest.

When we finally join the family on their land it has been three hours since we left the house. Three hours to cover the distance that, in normal, legal circumstances, used to take twenty minutes on foot.

And this is not the end of the journey. We still have to get to the olive trees we are to work on today. We get on the trailer again and F. takes us through stony paths that make both the tractor and the trailer bounce.

Fig 8: Israeli road next to Jayyous

For about half an hour we travel parallel to a road for the exclusive use of the Israelis, which is completely flat and perfectly asphalted and well-lit: nothing to do with the goats' path we have been bouncing along. There are also access gates to that fancy road. F. tells us that the fancy road has been constructed over a previously existing one, which was used by everyone, including himself and his family. It used to take them ten minutes to cover the distance that is taking us half an hour to cover now.

The Israeli road has a shoulder on each side, double the width of the road itself, made of soil and sand. The function of the perfectly flat sand on the hard shoulder is to record any footsteps of intruders on it. F. explains that it is checked and kept in the best of conditions at least twice a day. Fig 8

Indeed, this road, having a fence on each side, acts as a wall. Up to where we can see, there is a double fence with razor wire on the ground, in such a way that, if you try to cross it, first you get electrocuted with the first fence, or the electronic sensors detect you so that the soldiers can shoot you. If they do not kill you, you jump and you get wounded with the razor wire, and if you manage to jump the second fence with the barbed wire on it, your steps on the road shoulder give you away, and if you have not been shot dead yet, you will be now.

In theory all these barriers act as protection against Palestinian terrorists. In practice what is meant is to make life quite impossible for Palestinian farmers like F., who have to travel for two or three hours each time they go to their own lands.

When we finally get to F.'s land, we are in the area between the "Green Line" and the illegal wall, a band of about six kilometres wide between the internationally agreed border between the States of Israel and Palestine and the wall that the Israeli State is building inside Palestinian territory. The land belongs to Palestinian farmers and the United Nations say that this is Palestinian territory, that should become the Palestinian Country. But the Israeli government says it is Israeli territory. That is why Palestinians need special permission from the Israeli authorities to access their own land.

In the Israeli territories where the ownership of the land is no longer discussed, because it was either bought more or less legally or simply stolen so long ago the United Nations seem to recognise it as Israeli land, streets and roads are more than sufficiently lit. Just like in any western country. Not these lands. There is not a single lamp here so it is only possible to work while the sun is up. Taking into account that we have lost three hours dealing with the illegal fence, that permissions do not last for as many days as necessary, and that we did not have breakfast this morning, F. is in quite a bad mood and willing to make up for the lost time.

While we work, Abu A. and F. seem to realise that it is not practical to waste three hours in the morning and another three in the evening every day just so that we can help them. They decide that we will stay in a small shed that belongs to Abu A., still between the illegal fence and the Green Line. By the time we get to the shed all our bags, which we had left in F.'s house thinking we would stay there for a few more days, are here in the shed. We marvel and are grateful for the fact that nothing is missing from all the things we had left in the different rooms. There is also some dinner on the table and, although it is not as copious as yesterday's, we finish off just as full. There is also hot water prepared for us in the water tank, heated with a fire underneath it, just outside the shed, so we can have a shower, at least one of us each day. The only thing we will lack here is electricity. But we will have running water inside the house - and, if we want, hot water too - and we will not be hungry. Not all Palestinians have these luxuries.

Abu A. tells us about the water and its administration in this area during dinner. Palestinians have such strict limits on the amount of water they can use from their own wells, that they have to rotate the irrigation of their fields. Some fields are irrigated one year and the rest the second year, so each year only half of the land is cultivated. The inhabitants of the illegal Israeli settlement, however, use water from these same wells plentifully for their daily use, their swimming pools and their gardens, without having to worry about rotation. Palestinians are not even allowed to drill more wells in their own land. Abu A. sees the total water consumption from his land and he thinks the Israeli settlers waste water, or at least that they use it without control.

We ask him what would happen if he once decided to not respect the limit in water usage, and he answers that the soldiers would simply cut off all the pipes that conduct the water to the lands that are still in Palestinian hands. The Israeli army regularly checks the water consumption of the Palestinians, and has threatened not to allow them to use any of their own water if they go over the limit they have established. They have also had the right to drill more wells denied since the seventies. So while the illegal Israeli settlement grows and expands, no more wells can be drilled in Palestinian land, and the whole area, more than six square kilometres, together with the Israeli settlement, operates with the water of just five wells.

It is estimated that about a hundred houses are inhabited in the illegal Israeli settlement. But there are about five hundred houses, says Abu A. He then talks about a certain very rich Jewish man who lives abroad and finances houses in future Israeli settlements, whether there is demand for such houses or not. So most of these houses stay empty until someone decides to move in, like the case of the settlement near this land, where only a fifth of the houses are inhabited.

As if four hundred empty houses were not enough, now the plan is to build fifteen hundred (1,500) new houses. All this on Abu A.'s land. It is for the construction of these houses that Abu A.'s trees were uprooted, and it is for them that the Palestinians are not allowed to use the shortest routes to get into their own land. And we are talking about a settlement that is illegal right from its conception.

Abu A. tells us that last week the settlers put up flags around the confiscated land (which is not even officially confiscated because Abu A. is contesting this in court), in order to mark the expansion of the settlement. J. says that this is a method also used in the United States (he keeps calling them simply America) to indicate areas in new or planned construction.

Third Wednesday - **"The settlers took my land"**

We pick olives with F. and his family today as well. We have slept in this shed that lies between the Green Line and the illegal wall. They say it is only a security wall for the settlement, but instead of putting it next to the Israeli settlement, they have put it about six metres away from the last houses of the Palestinian village.

Since there is no gate for us to cross today, we can afford ourselves the luxury of sleeping until eight o'clock in the morning. Still this shed is quite far away from the area where we need to go, next to the settlement, and we still have to travel over a very rocky and rough path to get there.

It used to take F. only ten minutes to get to his land before the fence was built, when he could take paved roads for most of the way. Nowadays he has to cross the fence and then travel over this path, which actually follows the path of the fence with its nicely paved road next to it. It now takes him more than an hour to travel to his land, forced as he is to drive the entire distance over the rocks, even though there are paved roads and other gates from which we can see his land. But the nice roads are for Israelis only and the gates are closed for Palestinians.

Land confiscation has already happened in many areas. F.'s uncle points at the plot of land that used to be his family's property, explaining that it is now being used as farmland by the settlement inhabitants. F.'s nephew looks no older than ten, and he also has a story to tell: all the empty land that we can see from here used to be his father's. He says the settlers just took the land and they are using it now with the Army's protection. There are no olive trees planted on that land any more.

We will stay in the shed tonight again and, as we arrive, we find not only hot water ready for a shower, but also a nice fire outside the shed, next to the door.

It is customary for some Palestinians to sit outside their houses and light fires on special plates, with legs, as if they were small round tables. After a few hours, when the fire is smaller and produces no smoke, they bring it into the house and it heats at least the living room. Abu A. is there waiting for us and we all sit outside, around the fire, with him.

In the distance we can hear vague sounds of partying, and music that sounds like pop. It is the first time I hear western style music in Palestine. Abu A. says the party is in the Israeli settlement, and in fact that is where the noise is coming from, not from the Palestinian village. He also says it sounds like they are getting drunk, or something of the like, in the settlement, and that this problem does not exist in Palestine because the Islamic religion forbids alcohol. However, because of the strangulation of the Palestinian economy by the Israeli State, there are serious drugs problems among the Palestinian youth.

It is also very frequent that we can hear, even where we are now, far away from the village, the calls to prayer from the village mosques. I have already got used to these calls. In a given moment, the call to prayer, usually sung, turns into a quick monologue. Abu A. asks us to stay silent with a gesture and listens carefully. When it finishes, he tells us it was an announcement that from tomorrow the gate opening times will change.

We look at him in astonishment - is this how the farmers can find out when they can or can not work on their lands? He explains: the soldiers are not always at the gates, and when a gate is unattended, it is closed. This is completely arbitrary, and they do not give any notice of it. Sometimes the soldiers may know what the opening hours will be the next day, but if you do not go through that gate on that day, or they simply do not remember to tell you, or they say they do not know, you go the next day only to find the gate closed, without soldiers and without information.

So today the Israeli army has decided to change the timetable of some gate, without previous notice, in fact, without any notice at all. Then the villagers themselves passed on the message to each other and the announcement is now made from the mosque for all to hear, to make sure that people will not get trapped on their own land tomorrow when the gate is closed an hour earlier at dusk.

Before we can recover and assimilate this information, Abu A. starts to sing songs against the occupation that, he says, are older than the current occupation.

"How come?", we ask.

"Look. My father was born under the Ottoman Empire occupation. I was born under the British Empire occupation. And my sons were born under the Israeli occupation. Such is life". And he says this with a wide smile, looking at us, expectant, as if expecting to see our smiles too. So I can just keep silent and smile.

Then I ask him if all the occupations were the same, if the Ottoman and British occupations were as brutal as this one.

"Of course they weren't. This one is the worst by far. The previous ones, they were just governments that happened to be foreign".

A conversation about politics follows. He tells us how much he respects us internationals who leave the comforts of our countries, and etc. etc. He says that our mere presence is the most important thing here, not how hard we work, picking olives or whatever. That is not important. The important thing is that we show our support. Our governments are the ones who should do something but, lacking that, at least they can see they are not alone in their plight.

"But, your governments", asks Abu A. without really expecting an answer, "why are they not doing anything for us, and against Israel? They have declared the wall illegal, the settlements illegal, the occupation illegal, why are they not doing anything?"

"Doing something would mean to stand up against the most powerful country in the world. And no government can afford or would dare to do that".

"Exactly", answers Abu A. with a wide smile. And he goes on about our very important mission here in Palestine and back home, telling what we have seen here.

He also says that, although what we are doing is a lot, he would ask us to do something more. He reminds us that a global boycott helped finish off the apartheid regime in South Africa, and if it worked there, it should work here too. He would like us to take this message back: boycott Israeli products so that its human rights abuses end, like boycott ended apartheid in South Africa.

Our answer goes that, unfortunately, there are a lot more economical interests in the support for Israel than there were for the support for South Africa.

"Exactly!", and he shakes his head with a smile on his face.

Third Thursday - **The Green Line**

Abu A. takes us on a "tour" around the area on the way to his groves today. We get on his tractor for that, so we endure a rocky path again, although today it is a different one. We then see a different portion of the fortified wall disguised as a fenced-off road.

Abu A. also shows us the single well from where water is drawn to irrigate all the land that we can see plus the illegal Israeli settlement. He stops the tractor and shows us the water meters. He explains that the Israeli soldiers check the Palestinians' water usage often, at least once a week.

He also shows us the permit that allows him but not his sons nor his wife to access his land through specific gates. The permit is written only in Hebrew, which is a bit of a shock, bearing in mind that it is for a Palestinian, and that in cities like Jerusalem all sign posts are written in Hebrew, Arabic and English. He explains to us what is included on the permit paper: the name of the person who is allowed through the gate, the number of the specific gate, the dates they are allowed to get through, whether they are allowed to spend the night on their land or not... Most farmers are not allowed to stay overnight on their own lands.

Some of these farmers understand Hebrew, if they have previously worked in Israel. But this document is not meant to be a means of communication between the State and the farmers; it is just a means of communication between the Israeli authorities and the soldiers, about the Palestinians.

So if one day the soldier says that according to this document they can not get through any gate, the Palestinians can not even contest it - even if they can speak Hebrew and can discuss it, Abu A. says. Each soldier is an official, and whatever will be allowed that day depends on that day's soldier's mood.

We get on the tractor again and Abu A. takes us to the Green Line, where the wall should stand if Israel respected the treaties it has signed. The distance is so big in some parts that the Green Line can not be seen from the actual wall. In this part, the "wall" is secured by two barbed wire fences separated by a few feet of razor wire coils. One of the fences appears to be electrified, or at least it has some kind of electronic sensory equipment.

When we arrive at his land we get a surprise because there are no olive trees, only orange trees. He explains that he used to have vegetables, but with all that gates and permission business his vegetables got rotten in the soil because he was not allowed to enter his own land when they needed watering or were ready to be harvested, so he planted trees. Trees do not need so much attention and regular care.

We harvest two full buckets of mandarins each and Abu A. insists that we keep a good few of them. Then we go to where the uprooted olive trees used to be, the ones on the pictures of the first night. Today, small shoots of new trees are peeking through the ground from the remnants of the root systems. They look like newly planted trees.

There are quite a few people in the shed when we get back there, just before dark. O., a Jewish Israeli, has brought people who will take over from us here. We will probably leave tomorrow but tonight we are having a nice family meal that Abu A.'s wife has cooked at home.

As an Israeli citizen, O. has a car with an EU-looking number plate with the "I" for Israel on it that gives him access to the Israeli, perfectly asphalted roads, and the right to go through checkpoints without getting out of his car.

Like us, he uses his privileges to try to make Palestinians' lives a bit more bearable. Unlike us, he has been doing this every day for years, not just for a few weeks or months like us.

The rest of the people at the table are members of CCPT who have known Abu A. and his wife for some time now. G. makes a comment about the amount of food that Abu A. is giving us. Abu A. explains a bit about his Islamic religious obligations to make three parts of everything he ever receives, giving one third to the poor and sharing another third, and this is the third part of a camel he has been given that he is sharing with us.

We then talk about what we have seen today and J. summarises at the end:

"All the settlements on the Palestinian side of the 'Green Line' are illegal according to the Geneva Conventions, which prohibit occupation forces from transferring their civil population to occupied territories. And the United Nations have clarified that the West Bank and Gaza are occupied territories and therefore Israel should submit to the international law on occupied territories."

"Yes, but when has Israel honoured international treaties, including those that it has signed?"

Third Friday - **Israeli treats**

I wake up before daylight and go out of the shed. There is a bit of light coming out of the back of the distant mountains, but the sun is still hidden behind them. There is a very special orange-green colour in the sky, just above the mountain, that becomes bluer higher up from the mountains and into the rest of the sky. Slowly, it gets lighter and lighter and the stars disappear in the daylight. The air is deliciously fresh and clean. I go back to the shed and I meet J. outside it; he had gone out to see the dawn as well, and is now coming back, ready to prepare breakfast for everyone.

While we prepare breakfast together we agree that we should ask O. for a lift to get out of the "realms" of this settlement and then make ourselves available to go wherever we may be needed, now that people from the EAPPI are taking over here in Jayyous.

Everyone comes out of the shed called by the smell of food and we all have breakfast. O. will take us to his house so we can use his washing machine and his shower. We were not expecting this offer even remotely. Shower and washing machine!

After breakfast we say good bye and leave with O.

In a car with an Israeli number plate now and with an Israeli citizen at its wheel, we get absolutely no trouble at the gate. O. is free to choose the most convenient gate to drive to the city where he lives. We quickly get on to an Israeli road, very similar to any "A" road in the UK, only this one has hills on each side of the road as if a small mountain had been cut in the middle in order to build it. O. explains that they do that when building the roads where only Israeli citizens will be allowed to drive, so that they will not see the conditions in which the Palestinians are made to live - with their "rocky roads", as J. had politely put it, the "vehicles" they are allowed to drive, and the sheds they use as houses after demolitions.

Once in his house, he lets us use his electricity, his computer, his internet, his washing machine, his shower and his sofas. This gets us ready for our next trip. Tomorrow J. and I are going to a village in the mountains, to the North of Nablus, where the settlers from the local illegal settlement threw all the local Palestinians out years ago, by terrorising them, especially at night. They would invade their village in the middle of the night destroying whatever they could, they poisoned their well, the only source of water for the whole village, and they burnt the electric generator, that the United Nations had donated to them. They would stone whoever would get in their way and a killing happened. The inhabitants fled the village and there was a lot of local and international media attention, but, knowing that when this faded away they would be faced with the same terror situation, they only agreed to go back to the village on condition that there would be a continuous international presence. Usually this continuous presence is provided by the EAPPI, but these days they are having a meeting of all the people "deployed" in Palestine and the people stationed here also wanted to attend. So they have asked us to "cover" Yanoun while they are in this meeting. This is our next "assignment".

Third Saturday - **Yanoun**

As O. drives us to the nearest town to Yanoun, Aqraba, he tells us about the latest incident that happened there. A settler injured a Palestinian farmer and he is luckily alive, recovering in hospital.

We get out of O.'s car in Aqraba and he continues his trip after arranging for a taxi to pick us up. We wait right at the spot where he leaves us, with our bags on the ground, on the side of the road. Next to us there is a small stone wall. A few metres away from us, also next to the wall, about six or seven men are sitting on chairs in a semicircle. Of course our presence does not go unnoticed. They ask us where we are from and then tell us that the taxi O. has arranged should be here in ten or fifteen minutes. Then another man appears as if from nowhere and offers us two chairs that we can not refuse.

Then yet another man, more elderly than all the rest, with a kheffiyeh over his head, approaches us. First he asks J. where he comes from, and then he asks:

"And your companion, where is she from?" J. lets me answer. He tells us he is the Mayor of Aqraba and the conversation takes political and religious paths. He asks J. whether he believes in God and J. says he is not religious. The man seems to find it difficult to understand that someone does not believe in God. He asks J. a few more questions trying to understand and then he asks me. When I say yes, he sighs, in relief, as if saying: "Well, at least it is not both of them".

Then he asks J. what he has studied. He answers up to Secondary School. The man insists, so we guess he is referring to University.

"No, I did not go to University", says J. The face of the man says that he does not understand:

"But all Americans go to University. Why you did not go to University?"

"I come from a poor background."

"Poor?" The man scratches the kheffiyeh on his head as if saying to himself: "Let's see if I can understand this". We look at him, rather amused. "Poor in America?"

J. and I bite our lower lips. We explain that in America, and all over the world, there are poor people, not just in countries like this. I suspect the man either can not understand it, or can not believe us, or both.

The Palestinian people have been seeing foreigners, mainly from the USA, for many years; people who have been coming in solidarity, like us. The good consequence is that they are able to distinguish between the governments and the governed. The bad consequence is that, having had contact only with those who come, they have been getting these misleading ideas that all western people, especially those from the US, are vegetarians and have gone to University.

So they are now faced with the very different story of J., who is indeed a vegetarian but has spent two years working and saving up to pay for this trip, and has never been to University. One stereotype they have formed over the years thanks to the stories of the people they have met has just gone out of the window.

J. asks him about the event of a few days ago. The mayor tells us that the injured man is an acquaintance of his, a cousin. He was on his land harvesting his olives when a settler, a man with a rifle, came up to him. The farmer picked up a stone in an instinctive move to defend himself. Palestinians are not allowed to have weapons, even at home, and can not carry knives in the street, but the settlers are allowed, and even encouraged, to carry big machine guns hanging from their shoulders, and there are reports that these weapons are financed by the Israeli government for the settlers.

The settler shouted something like:

"What are you doing on my land!" and the farmer told him that it was his land, that his family had had it for generations, and that he had come to pick his olives, like every year. The settler screamed at him again saying that the land was his by divine right, since the Bible says it, and that the Palestinian had no right to step on it.

At this point the farmer threw the stone to the ground, away from the settler, and then the settler, with the back of his rifle, hit him strongly on the face, making a large wound, and he had to be taken to hospital.

"He has been in hospital for ten days now", says the mayor of Aqraba.

During his speech I have taken out my camera and have tried to record his words. The mayor has become more and more solemn since he realised that a camera was filming. We tell him that we are not journalists, that we will try to get this out in our own circles, but he just goes on in his dignified mayoral pose, explaining...

When the taxi finally comes, we give the chairs back and we say goodbye to all the men. The mayor offers us his house to come and eat whenever we want to, but, our function being to stay in Yanoun in order to try our best to avoid incidents like the one just related, we are not able to accept his offer.

The taxi takes us through a very narrow road that is the only access to Yanoun from Palestinian territory. The road is tiny, but recently asphalted. The taxi driver tells us that it was a path before, until a Saudi Arabian bank financed the asphalting works.

We arrive at the "international flat" in Yanoun. There are three internationals here already, but two of them are leaving tomorrow and there should always be at least two internationals here. They explain the situation in Yanoun.

The village is situated on one face of a hill, which is itself surrounded by two other hills that leave a long valley between them. The road to Lower Yanoun and Aqraba runs along that valley. The illegal Israeli settlement extends over the three mountains, although we can not see any houses from here. All we see from Yanoun is the soldiers' outposts and some barracks up on the mountains at each side of this one, in such a way that the village is observed from right and left, and probably from above too.

During the night there are two very powerful light beams, illuminating the village so that the soldiers, and probably the settlers too, can have a clear view of the village all night. As for the streets themselves, the lighting is very poor, financed by charity, too.

The limits of the area we can walk are very clear. To go to Lower Yanoun, internationals and Palestinians must always stay on the road. We can wander to the lands to the right of it, but not to the ones on the left. The mountain on the left is a no-go area for all but Israelis. On the mountain to our right there is the house of a Palestinian family and that is the limit; we must not go any further. And, up this mountain, a few rocks are the "border". If we do not respect these limits, we could be shot at from the outposts.

Our functions here are to stay visible, to visit the village's families, and to call certain Israeli authorities and activists if we see settlers approach the well or the new electricity generator.

In a normal country, the logical thing to do would be to call the police in emergency situations. Here, if the Palestinians approached the outposts asking for help, the soldiers would detain them and get them arrested. If the Palestinians dared to confront the settlers who destroy the things they need to live, they would probably get shot.

L. tells us the story of a man who was walking down the road to Aqraba and was approached by two soldiers. They told him to go to the other side of the road and he refused, knowing that it is forbidden for Palestinians to go on that side. The soldiers insisted and he overhead one of them saying in Hebrew that the first thing to do if he did obey and go to the other side of the road would be to detain him and get the police to properly arrest him for going to the forbidden side of the road. He then insisted that he could not go to that side of the road, and they arrested him for disobeying them.

There are some Israeli organisations in contact with this project, like "Rabbis for Human Rights". One of them has made himself available for this village for any emergency, even at night. This is because if a Palestinian or a foreigner calls the authorities, they will not move a finger, but it is different if it is an Israeli calling them.

L. takes us to the house of one of the local families and after a few seconds of talking we are invited for dinner - a few small dishes of hummus, olive oil, tomato sauce, eggs, zahtar, olives... L. has been around for a few months now and is learning Arabic, so a conversation in Arabic is established in one corner of the floor-made-table with him while English is spoken in the rest of the room.

As usual, we get some of the history of the village from its inhabitants: Three or four years ago the settlers started a campaign of "night raids" into the village, terrorising the Palestinian villagers, coming with white hoods, in Ku Klux Klan fashion. On one of those occasions they bathed in the only well that provides all the water this village uses, and they bathed their dogs too, to make the water completely unusable. They also destroyed their electricity generator, which had been paid for by some United Nations charity programme. The settlers said that no one had asked them for permission to install it, therefore it was their duty to destroy it. All this happened, the family tell us, while the soldiers stood by, doing nothing apart from laughing. The settlers eventually killed one of the Palestinian villagers and all the families decided to leave. The whole village was empty except for two people who did not have any family that could house them elsewhere.

There was a lot of media hype about it. Local and foreign media came, and then the internationals came. The Palestinians wanted to return to their village to lead normal lives, not to look out to the top of the hill in fear of the settlers. So they asked the internationals to stay and protect them, if only with their presence, which seems to be enough, even though all we have are cameras and our words and our privileges as citizens of rich countries as our weapons, as opposed to the soldiers' and settlers' M16s.

They tell us that some settlers told the Palestinians that the journalists would eventually leave and so would the internationals, but they, the settlers, would always stay. But the internationals have not left since then, and although we can not prevent punctual events like the last one from happening, life has gone on relatively peacefully in the village, apart from the occasional harassment or attack from settlers or soldiers.

One of the many children of the family, a beautiful little girl, keeps looking at me almost in amazement and at one point I ask her:

"What is your name?"

A very basic conversation follows between her and me and she asks me to go to school with her tomorrow.

We eventually leave the house and come back to the international flat, take a rest and talk about what the locals have told us. I tell L. about the girl's idea of me going to school and he encourages me to accept her invitation. He says the local people will actually appreciate my presence there. In fact L. goes to the village school every day, and talks with the teachers and plays with the pupils in the breaks. He also says that tomorrow's English lesson is at nine in the morning, which is the perfect time for us both to go and then stay for the rest of the day.

Third Sunday - **School in Yanoun**

J. and Z. stay at home while L. and I go to school at nine o'clock in the morning. L. has had a timetable mix-up; the English lesson is in a few hours time. L. goes to one classroom and I go to another one. This is the eldest children's classroom; next year they will have to travel to Aqraba every day to attend secondary school. I am attending an Arabic lesson.

I can not see any lights on the ceiling nor plugs in the walls; they do not seem to use electricity here. The windows are square holes in the walls, without any glass or frame. The doors stay open to let the light come through.

In total there are three classrooms and also a kitchen in the school. Two levels are taught in each classroom by each teacher, both at the same time, so only six years are taught here. There are also children from Lower Yanoun, who come in the daily shuttle van that also carries the older children to Aqraba for secondary school.

There is a computer in a corner at the end of the classroom. Whoever donated it, did not ask if there was electricity in the school.

Against the walls are various sets of shelves. They are full of boxes with the Unicef logo on them. All the children have the same model of school bag, with the same colours, and all their books look pretty old except for the English and Maths books. The English book is the only one that is opened as books are opened in the Western world. Its title is "English for Palestine". The rest of their books start where a western book would end and their titles are in Arabic.

During the break L. plans to play football with the kids and we both head for the playground, which consists of the road and a small esplanade next to it. The teachers, which are all men, tell him to stay in the kitchen for some lunch and he looks at me - the invitation is supposed to include me but they will talk to both of us through him, as is culturally mandatory. Lunch consists of a dish of oil, another dish of hummus and bread to dip in it. And, of course, tea.

They ask where I come from and they say that the van that takes the children to school was bought thanks to a Spanish-French charity organisation. The English teacher says that the children in this village are a lot better at English than those in Aqraba, thanks to their daily contact with internationals.

After the break there is finally the English lesson. The technique is a lot more "oral" and less academic than the way I was taught, but it looks a lot more useful, judging from how well young people speak English, even though they have never left this country - mainly because the Israeli authorities do not allow them to.

When school finishes, a white van with seats but no sign that it is a taxi comes from the same road we came on and the children who do not live in Upper Yanoun get in it. I guess this is the van the teachers talked about during the break. L. explains that it is the daily shuttle to and from Aqraba, mainly for the older children who have to go to the bigger city to attend the equivalent of secondary school, but also to take the children from Lower Yanoun to and from school in Upper Yanoun.

I find this schooling system quite similar to rural Spain, or at least a combination of what was the practice years ago and what is done now. Decades ago, in many small Spanish villages, the only teacher in the village would teach all the children of different ages in the same classroom. What they do now is run shuttles like this to bring pupils to bigger towns where they can attend school with more children their age. Which is partly what is done here, with children of two different ages joined in the same classroom, studying two different levels. Then the fact that these children need a shuttle bus to go to school every day is not because of the occupation, but because it is a rural area with small villages.

"Yes, it is easy to blame all the problems on the occupation", says L.

When school finishes we go home and then visit some families. L. seems to know most, if not all of them. He says it is best to visit as many different families as possible, because it is their knowledge of our presence that makes them feel safe.

We sit around the fires at the entrance of as many houses as we can visit, with the men of each house. At the last one, a woman in a long black dress and with her head covered sits next to the door, out of the circle that has formed around the fire, and looks at me. I smile at her and then she asks:

"Are you good at English?"

I make a face and she continues very serious and, staring at me, without blinking, she asks, almost states:

"Would you help my daughter".

I say I would and she invites me in, leaving all the men outside and taking me inside, with her daughters and younger sons. I immediately feel privileged to have been invited to a domestic realm where my male companions are not allowed.

The living room consists of a medium-sized room with a carpet and some thin, gymnasium-like mattresses to sit down on. In one of the corners there is a small piece of furniture with the children's books and notepads on its shelves and a TV set on top. In another corner there is a wardrobe with blankets. This is all their furniture. The children sit on the carpet or on the thin mattresses, as they watch TV or do their homework, using the same carpet they are sitting on as their studying table.

The mother introduces me to the daughter I have agreed to help and we both sit down on the carpet, while the mother goes to the kitchen. I realise that she speaks English better than me so I wonder what exactly she should need me for. She tells me that she has not actually prepared today's lesson because she has another exam tomorrow and, could I come back the day after tomorrow, after she has had her exam and prepared her lesson with questions for me.

I say I will and then the mother, who is now wearing a modern, colourful western tracksuit and has her hair tied up in a pony tail, invites me into the kitchen to eat.

There are fresh vegetables and falafel on the table for me. She tells me she makes the falafel herself and after we finish she gives me all the balls left to take home. I join the rest outside and after a few moments we the internationals go home. L. and Z. will take the shuttle that takes the older children to school in Aqraba at about eight o'clock tomorrow morning. They are going to some other place in need of internationals.

FOURTH WEEK

Fourth Monday - **Not enough of us**

J. and I stay in Yanoun. He does not fancy going to school so I go on my own. The relationship between me and the teachers, without a man to accompany me, is completely different today. The teachers say hello briefly to me and avoid me as much a possible.

In class, the teachers do try to include me in the dynamics, the English teacher especially. He asks the pupils questions about Spain and they all say that it is in Europe and that its capital is Madrid, and that it has olive trees, like Palestine, and that some words are the same in Arabic and Spanish.

When school finishes it is midday and I feel like walking in the sun, so J. and I go to visit Lower Yanoun for the rest of the day. The unwritten but strict rules say that the Palestinians and internationals must not step out of the mountain where the village stands, or they may be killed. The settlers are armed and they are not usually arrested when they assault Palestinians. If caught when they kill one, the penalty, if there is one, is always laughable. So J. and I walk on the road without stepping off it. We are white and privileged but we have not come here to create problems.

When we arrive in Lower Yanoun a girl shouts, "Hello!" from a distance, running towards us. When she gets nearer she tells us that her mother wants us to visit her house. We follow the girl and she guides us, first climbing over some rocks, then into a bare stone construction through a hole in the wall, then again climbing over more rocks. They are laid in disorder one on top of the other. As we climb up, they become something like a staircase and we reach an opening to our left. We go through it and we are then inside a covered bare patio/corridor with nothing but entrances like this one on both sides. Some of them have curtains down to knee-level, but there are not any proper doors or windows, not even frames, and the wind blows everywhere.

The girl guides us into one of those entrances and takes off her shoes. We do the same, as we do in every house. The room we enter is also made of stone, like the patio. There is a TV set in a hole in the wall, a small table, a chair and a couple of mattresses. This is their living room and this is all their furniture. There is a woman and a small child. They must be the mother and the brother of the girl who has taken us here. The whole place is quite windy; the wind comes through the window - which is just a hole in the wall, no frame, no glass - and goes out the door to the rest of the house. We look of out the window when the woman leaves and we see that we are roughly on the equivalent of a fifth floor from the street level.

The mother returns with some food for J. and me and, after a bit of conversation, she asks us to go with her children to a nearby mountain to bring some lunch to their father. Usually she brings it herself while her children take the sheep and goats to the fountain, but now that we are here she would feel a lot safer if the children go to the mountains with us as she tends the animals, instead of leaving the children in the village alone.

The girl, J. and I start what is supposed to be a ten minute walk. Between us three, we are carrying some glasses, a few empty plastic bottles and a covered tray. The first stop is the village fountain, to fill the plastic bottles with water. More children join us at the fountain and they explain to us that there is no water inside the houses. I look up towards the settlement in the certainty that there is not a single house there without cold and hot water supply inside, heating and lots of furniture.

The fountain is right on the side of an old road and we continue walking on it. Suddenly an army vehicle that looks more like a tank than a car appears from nowhere and we all freeze at the side of the road, looking at each other and at the vehicle. It is a compact thing, made of brown metal with wheels that can not be seen. We can not see passengers or drivers either.

We remain frozen while the vehicle passes besides us and, once it is out of sight, the children simply continue walking. Clearly, these children are more used to this kind of vehicle than us. The girl looks at me, smiles and exhales a deep breath; luckily nothing has happened this time.

I do not even take my camera out to take a picture of this vehicle, because every time one takes a picture of anything from the military - a checkpoint, an outpost, a soldier even - one is risking, if not one's life, at least the camera, the tapes and all the content taken so far. Or maybe it is because its appearance was too sudden and we were too frozen.

We continue walking on the side of the road and then start climbing the mountain where the children's father is. After fifteen minutes of the children saying: "Near" every time we ask where he is, they shout: "There!".

J. goes on climbing with the boys and I sit down on a rock with the girl. Their father is with two other men and the three of them are throwing trunks down the hill. It is the wood they will be using in the winter to heat their houses, the girl explains.

J. helps them with the trunks, the children leave the food with the rest of the men's things and, after a few minutes, most of the children are sitting with me. I tell them that the view from here is beautiful and one of the boys tells me:

"All this land, my father's. Settlers steal it".

I move my head waiting for a bit of a clearer explanation and he goes on:

"One day, settler says, 'it's mine'", and he shrugs his shoulders. So that's it. End of the story. I take some pictures of the land he is indicating and I realise that it is actually the best portion of land I can see around, right in the valley, flat and easy to work on. The rest is on the hills where we are sitting now, rocky, hilly and with the trees a lot more scattered than down there in the valley. Fig 9

I guess that is the explanation. They lose their livelihood to a fanatic, armed settler, and they try to get by with tree trunks for heating. I also guess they lost, sold or burned all their furniture, doors and windows in the process, and that is probably why the houses are so bare.

J. and the men throw the trunks down the hill for almost half an hour after they eat. We should not be this far away from the houses and the rest of the neighbours for too long so we excuse ourselves and leave.

Once at home, J. receives a call asking us to leave Yanoun and go to Bi'Lin, where there has been a violent incursion by the Israeli Army. Someone is needed there quickly because there is no international presence there at the moment. It is not at all surprising that the Army has done this on a day when there were no internationals there. After all, what we are here for is mostly to monitor actions like these, exactly the kinds of things that the Army do not want to be known.

Apparently here in Yanoun it has been pretty quiet in the last two weeks since the last attack, which makes some people think that our presence here is not so indispensable any more, or at least not as necessary as in Bi'Lin. J. and I discuss this and reach the conclusion that if we leave this village empty, the same or a similar thing can happen here. But J. would also rather leave the inactivity here to go to the demonstration in Bi'Lin, where he thinks he can be more effective.

Apparently the incursion in Bi'Lin was especially nasty and there is pressure for us to leave this place in order to "cover" Bi'Lin. But I think that if we both leave Yanoun it would contribute to the possibility of incursions here.
J. and I decide to go and see the Mayor of Yanoun and ask him what he thinks. His English is not too fluent but it is enough to ask us to stay.

"Two, better than one", he says. He fears that there will be incursions here if only one of us stays. He says the Israeli army will know how many of us are here because they are observing the village all the time from the outpost, on the top of the hill.

Nothing of importance has happened so far, but, again, if nothing happens it is probably thanks to our presence. I begin to suspect that our presence here must be quite uncomfortable for these fanatics, who can not continue to terrorise the Palestinian population as they would like to, just because there are some foreigners who take pictures and videos of human rights abuses. How inconvenient.

J. thinks it is a good compromise to leave one person here while the other leaves. He wants to get to Bi'Lin in time for the demonstration, so he packs his things in order to leave early tomorrow morning on the school shuttle. We say goodnight and goodbye, sure that we will see each other again around the occupied lands.

Fourth Tuesday - **"Are you on your own?"**

When the villagers decided to leave Yanoun after the terror campaign carried out by the local settlers, they were then "convinced" to come back to live here. They agreed, only on the condition that at least two or three internationals would be here at all times. The organisation called CCPT took on the commitment of keeping at least three people here at all times.

Today we are breaking this rule as J. leaves early in the morning. We all hope that it will go unnoticed at the outpost on the hill. I am assured by CCPT that two people will come tonight, so at least this place will be left with just one international for less than 24 hours. Being the only one here then, I decide against going to the school today and remain contactable in the flat and the surroundings instead, in case anything happens.

In the evening, just as I am getting ready for the English lesson I promised two days ago, there is a knock on the door of the international flat. It would not be the first time that the Israeli Army has tried to get into this flat so I go into alert mode immediately. There is a second knock as gentle or more than the first one and I relax a bit. The caller is a young Palestinian man with a little boy. When I open the door, the man explains that he is from Aqraba but now lives in the United States, where he is studying at university. Now he is on vacation visiting his family and is leaving tomorrow, and his family would like to invite us for dinner tonight, while he is here.

In normal circumstances I would have invited them in, but one strict rule is that Palestinians are not allowed in this flat, the same as Israelis are not allowed. The young man seems to understand even before I attempt to explain it and the conversation goes on with me in the flat and them on the street.

Fig 9: Stolen valley

65

I tell him I am on my own but even if I was not, we would not go for dinner as far away as Aqraba, leaving Yanoun on its own. He seems to be stuck on my first phrase:

"Are you here on your own?", he asks, with his eyes wide open.

I say yes but quickly add:

"I'm expecting two more people tonight".

He still points out:

"You shouldn't be here on your own".

I tell him I have to visit one of the village families in five minutes and he leaves. I put my shoes on and go to the house of the girl I am going to help with her English. Her mother receives me, looking worried:

"Are you on your own?" - she asks dryly. It seems news travels fast, I guess like in any other village. I explain that someone is expected to arrive later today, but she just continues to look worried.

I answer her daughter's queries as best as I can while we have a light dinner and then I return to the flat, which does indeed feel very lonely.

A few hours later, C. and X., from CCPT, turn up in a private taxi. I sincerely welcome the company and I update them about the past few days, fortunately not having anything special to report.

X. goes to bed and C. stays up, and he explains to me what I partly knew, that we have momentarily covered for CCPT here so they could all go to this Palestine-wide meeting, which is now over. They, C. and X., will now be here for a few weeks at least, maybe months.

He explains that some people stay here in Yanoun for three months, which is the full length of time that CCPT people stay in Palestine. I ask him how come so many people can afford to stay for so long. He says CCPT is an ecumenical program, carried out by a union of different Christian churches, and that it is most successful in Sweden and the United States. Indeed most people we have met here from the CCPT are Swedish.

"And people's jobs?", I ask. He explains that the norm in Sweden is for companies to keep people's jobs open. I look at him with envy and wonder aloud if I could get into something like this, and he points out that the Roman Catholic Church does not participate in this.

The conversation moves on to how we are assimilating the experience here in Palestine and of course we talk about the cultural differences. He tells me about a small past incident between a bunch of young Palestinian boys, a female international and himself. All the Palestinian boys stretched out their hands to the girl, smiling, trying to shake hands with her, and she refused, without a word. He thought at the time that she was being rude to the boys so he shook all their hands. When the moment had passed, he asked the girl why she had been so rude, and she explained that it was them that had been rude. The Palestinian rule is that a man does not attempt to touch or shake hands with a woman unless she makes the first move - this we have all been told. To make such an attempt is to consider her an "easy girl", and to insist in stretching out their hands in order to reach hers is an outright insult. So the boys were actually insulting her, and the fact that they were all smiling showed that all they intended to do was to make fun of her. Therefore her reaction, refusing to shake hands and smile, was the correct one.

We agree that Palestinian men seem to think we western women are all what they would call "easy", because they think we are like the women that the western mainstream media portray, especially Hollywood films. And we have seen that Hollywood films sell well on local television.

C. shows contempt for this perception the Palestinians have of western women. He relates this to the Palestinian complaint that western people think they are all terrorists just because the media portray them as such, and then it is them that buy into the western media stereotypes.

C. suggests watching one of the films he has got on DVD and we choose "War Lord", starring Nicolas Cage. Cage's character fancies a woman that he has only seen in street posters. After he gets to know her, it takes just three scenes to see them together in bed.

After the film C. goes to the men's room to sleep. I stay up packing, trying to not make too much noise. Tomorrow morning I am getting the school shuttle and leaving Yanoun.

It takes me a few minutes after I go to bed to actually fall asleep. Maybe that is why I am the only one in the flat to hear X. moan from the other room in his sleep. I walk to their door, half-open it and whisper:

"Are you OK?" He says nothing. I imagine he is too embarrassed to say anything and prefers to just shut up, or maybe I have not even woken him up, so I return to my bed.

A few minutes later, he starts to shout in desperation, almost crying. It is the kind of cry that comes out with the mouth shut, when something or someone is keeping the mouth shut forcibly. I walk to the men's room wondering if C. is just not hearing, not caring, or too doubtful as to what to do. Or maybe he is just too fast asleep.

I walk up to X.'s bed and I continue whispering. His shouts grow louder and more desperate and I decide it is time to wake him up. I touch him on the shoulder and he screams in panic and his body shakes violently; his arms just want to hit whatever it is that is attacking him, hitting just me, randomly, while his body shakes, and my arms try to stop his hitting me. I scream:

"It's me!! Wake up!!!"

He wakes up, stops waving his arms around and looks at me in wonder. I just manage to say:

"You were having a nightmare. Are you ok?" and he says something like:

"Yeah, I am, now".

He explains that many years ago he used to have the same nightmare regularly, with someone keeping him down and him trying to shout, but no sound coming out of his throat. Then he stopped having this nightmare for many years, and it is only now, here in Palestine, that he is having it again. I guess this stress that we all have and we never talk about is getting on us all, whether we notice it or not. But at least we are only here for a few months and then we go back home.

Fourth Wednesday - "**Do not move**"

I get the school shuttle to Aqraba to head South. In Lower Yanoun, the van picks up the children who are too old to go to the school in Upper Yanoun and takes them to Aqraba. The girl who invited us to her house and then guided us to her father, on the mountain, is among them. Only today she looks a lot older, in her uniform, her shoes and her hijab, unlike that afternoon, when she was wearing sandals and trousers and there was nothing hiding her long plaits.

In Aqraba I get on a normal taxi and then a regular coach service to get to Nablus, which is an important city, but it is in a state that it is difficult to describe with any other phrase than "state of siege". Five roads meet here, and there is a permanent checkpoint on each of them. None of those checkpoints is between Palestinian and Israeli territories. They are all in the middle of Palestine. The one I need to get through is about five or ten kilometres away from Nablus. At least it is not one we have to cross on foot. But the queue of vehicles is painfully slow and many people prefer to leave their taxis behind and then walk; it looks a lot faster. Others prefer to get a taxi right before the checkpoint instead.

An ambulance approaches the checkpoint from the opposite side with its emergency lights on, facing us. The cars in the queue make some space for the ambulance so that it can jump the queue. I expect that the soldiers will allow it to go past the checkpoint fast, but I am mistaken. One of the soldiers gets the driver's documents and another one gets in through the back door. None of them show any urgency, they just take their time, probably even more so than with any other vehicle. I sit there thinking that some one could be dying inside, desperately needing to get to hospital, but the soldiers slowly look into every possible part of the ambulance until they finally let it go. They could say that a terrorist could be hiding inside. The ambulance puts its siren on once it has gone through the checkpoint. I guess it is strictly forbidden to approach the checkpoint with sirens on.

They thoroughly check every vehicle going in both directions: the small carts pulled by donkeys or men, full of fruit and vegetables, the lorries with construction materials, the taxis full of people, and the very few private cars. They check the drivers' identities, the car boot, the load. They spend at least five minutes with each car, at least during the time I am here looking from my seat at the front of this coach.

After about an hour advancing a few metres every ten minutes, we get to the front of the queue. I do not think we will be stopped: One of the advantages of travelling on a big coach, they say, is that they do not tend to stop it and check and question everyone about their reasons for travelling, what they plan to do in their city of destination and what they have been doing in their city of departure, or what they are generally doing in this country where "there are men with guns, you know" (and what exactly are you, soldier, apart from a man with a machine gun?).

A soldier indicates to the driver to stop at the side of the road. Some other soldier then comes to the side of the coach and, with a severe look on his face and a motion of his hand, orders the driver to open the door. The driver will be about forty years old. The soldiers are no older than twenty and have a huge machine gun each. The soldiers' eyes are fixed on the driver.

One of the soldiers orders the driver to get out of the coach, again without talking, just with a slight motion of his hand. Of course the driver obeys immediately, without meeting the soldiers' eyes. The atmosphere is tense inside the coach. The driver and the soldiers exchange a few words in a language that sounds like Hebrew. The driver gets back on the coach, picks up the microphone and speaks in Arabic. As he puts the microphone down, when he finishes, he looks at me saying "Do not move" with his eyes and his hand. I nod.

Men of all ages start to walk down the aisle and then down the stairs. The soldier gets everyone's identity card as they get off the coach with their hand luggage. Another soldier comes to help and sees that the Palestinians are all at a reasonable distance from the soldiers, extending his arm and pushing the Palestinians that get "too near". He acts as if it is the armed soldiers that are the potential victims of these unarmed Palestinians, and not the other way round.

Once all the male passengers have handed over their identity cards and are all standing in front of the two soldiers, the one with the cards starts to call out their names, one by one.

One by one, as they are called out, the Palestinians open their bags on the ground, showing all their contents and answering the soldiers' questions before getting their papers and their things back and being allowed back onto the coach. The operation has taken about twenty minutes. But we are not done yet.

A soldier gives an order and the driver opens the boot where the bigger luggage is. From where I am I can see a soldier getting into the boot and then out again. I do not believe that in the three seconds that the expedition has lasted the soldier has had the time to open all the bags, see all their contents, check that none of them is a bomb and then put all the contents back in. So I wonder what use it is for security to check just the hand luggage of only the male passengers if they do not check anything else - if I could still buy the tale that this is about security. If it really were about security, they would buy scanners and they would not need so many soldiers around, it could even make economic sense. But so far the Israeli army has amply shown me that all this paraphernalia has nothing to do with security and everything to do with making the lives of Palestinians simply unbearable, with constant humiliations, with their looks, their manners, their arrogance, their roadblocks, their checkpoints, their M16s and the hours they make them waste even when they are inside an ambulance.

After failing to check all the big luggage and half of the hand luggage on the coach and delaying us for about an hour in the process, the coach is allowed to continue its journey. The passenger in front of me looks at me and tells me in English:

"This is the occupation".

I try to be sympathetic and answer:

"I know".

He answers back:

"You know?" as in, "What do you know about our situation, what can 'you' 'know'". And, thinking about it, he is most probably right. I have experienced it for a few weeks but from my privileged position I can barely imagine the hell these people have endured for as long as they can remember.

I keep my silence and the journey resumes.

Once on the other side of the checkpoint we see a long queue coming from the other direction: vehicles waiting to be checked, like we have been. I count four ambulances alongside the queue, all with their emergency lights on, all stuck in the queue. The road is not broad enough here for the rest of the vehicles to go to one side and allow them to jump the queue. So there they will stay, waiting for about half an hour each, waiting in the queue to be checked, like the rest of the vehicles, trying to run an emergency service to get ill people to hospital urgently.

When the coach gets to the end of its route we all get off. I ask around for the coaches to Ramallah and I get directed to a rather big coach station. Once there I see lots of empty coaches and just two drivers. I ask them for the coach to Ramallah but they do not know. Finally I find a family inside one of the coaches and I ask them:

"Do you speak English?"

The man says :

"No."

I insist:

"Ramallah?", expecting at least a yes or a no with his head. He gets off and walks with me to the exit of the station. He signals somewhere outside and says in English:

"Straight, left, then right".

I feel properly looked after by these people, who, not speaking English, do make the effort to help me find my way. I say "shukran" a couple of times and there I walk, away from this coach station, through streets that have no coaches or signs of them. When I finish going "straight, left, then right", and see no coaches, I feel completely lost. Suddenly I hear in the distance:

"Ramallah Ramallah!"

The man shouting is actually looking at me, and is standing beside a huge coach. So the man who did "not" speak English was absolutely right: the coaches that go to Ramallah do set off from here.

71

Fourth Thursday - **War crimes and deportations**

It is not too usual to see shootings in Ramallah nowadays. Especially since the compound of the Palestinian Authority, where Arafat used to live, was destroyed, there is virtually no Israeli military presence in the city. Now the Palestinian police can patrol the streets of Ramallah. They could not do that before because Ramallah was full of Israeli soldiers. The Israeli army regard all Palestinians as terrorists, or at least as potential terrorists. Palestinian police, like all police, carry arms, therefore for the Israeli State, they are armed terrorists, and therefore legitimate targets. And the Israeli judges, who are the only judges that exist in Israel and Palestine, and who would not be judges if they were not Zionists, will always find it justified if an Israeli soldier kills an armed policeman, that is to say an armed terrorist. Therefore no Palestinian police will ever be seen near or in view of Israeli soldiers.

And, although it is not frequent, we did see a shooting in Ramallah today.

I was in this first floor flat, not far away from the window, when we noticed a sudden movement of bodies outside, on the street, like people running, and trying to do so in silence. Then the shots.

"Tat - tat - tat - tat." Dry and quick, a lot less noisy than the simplest firecracker.

"Tat - tat - tat - tat." And then, again, this time nearer to the building where we were.

"Tat - tat - tat - tat."

By then all the internationals were stuck up against the windows, trying to figure out what was going on, trying to see. Until a voice near me shouted:

"Away from the window!!"

It is important to keep as far away as possible from the range of the bullets. Even if they are not aimed at you or your building, or your window. Those living in Palestine have already learned to feel no curiosity, but we internationals find it difficult to overcome ours. I guess we had imagined something like what we see in films and we wanted to see it with our own eyes.

But bullets have no glamour whatsoever. They do not even sound like bullets. And yet they can actually kill, or cause pain and a disability for the rest of your life. So you must stay away from the window, however curious you feel. Your physical integrity is far more important.

The next time I looked out, there were still men in uniform around, looking alert, but the shootings had ceased.

For the rest of the day, the shooting is not the most important theme of conversation. R., another "international" like us, has been arrested, and people are eager to hear the latest news about him.

From the information that is shared between the Israeli, the Palestinian and the international activists, it sounds like he was arrested while walking some school girls to school in Hebron, while he was waiting for his appointment to renew his visa. He would have been deported already if he had not challenged his own deportation. The result of this is that he will be held in a prison until he "changes his mind" and accepts his deportation.

I learn that one of the local papers has published a very misleading article, implying that he assisted terrorists a few years ago, in his previous visit to Palestine. Some of his friends are planning to write to the newspaper to contest this article. From their draft letter, I learn that the last action of R. in that first visit was to chain himself to a house that was due for demolition.

The Israeli forces demolish the houses of people accused of terrorism in order to punish their families too. There is no court case against the families, so there is no need to prove anything. It is enough to allege that they are the family of someone who has been named "a terrorist" in an Israeli martial court where the charges are unknown. This is called "collective punishment". It is condemned by the UN, and the Geneva Conventions call it a "crime of war". But there is no international force in Israel and international law is completely ignored.

R. used his body to try to prevent a crime of war from happening and the paper described this as "staying in a terrorist's house". The response of the Israeli forces at the time was to deport him - for trying to prevent collective punishment, a war crime.

After that, he could not return to Palestine, because any foreigner who has been arrested in Palestine, or has been deported, is banned from both countries for life. But R. changed his name legally back in his country, and came back in order to continue to work for human rights in Palestine. Back here he was given a time-limited visa like every other foreigner. Before it ran out, he went to the appropriate authorities to have it renewed. Those authorities gave him an appointment for a date which was "after" that expiry date. This, he was told, is standard practice, and the mere fact that he was given this appointment meant that his visa was extended until that date. But now the Israeli authorities in Hebron say that he overstayed his visa and was in the country illegally and therefore they have to deport him. From a local jail he has been sent to another one, at the far end of the country, to the south, in the desert, near Egypt, and he will be deported from there. All the way, his friends say, he has been in isolation. "Incommunicado."

From Ramallah I go to Bi'Lin, which are so close together that there is no permanent military checkpoint on the road that links them. Permanent, there is none. But there are also what are called "flying checkpoints": Three soldiers block the road with a few rocks and their all-terrain vehicle, and a checkpoint is built.

Back in Europe, if a vehicle flashes its headlights, it means that it has just passed a police control. There must be a similar system here because suddenly the taxi in which I am travelling takes a local rocky road. I look out the window and I see that there are other cars following this one, and cars ahead too, avoiding the road. A Palestinian boy travelling in the taxi with us explains the "trick" with a smile on his face and of course offers us his house to stay. We have to decline this offer, at least for tonight, because we are needed in Bi'Lin rather urgently.

Fourth Sunday - **The Wall in Bi'Lin**

They are building a wall around Bi'Lin, the same wall that separates, in theory, "Israeli territory" from "Palestinian territory", but separates, in reality, "Palestinian people" from "other Palestinian people", and all from their places of work and education, and their lands, until they lose their jobs and their lands and virtually all contact with their relatives who live a mere few kilometres away.

We have been in Bi'Lin for a few days now. I was in this village at the very beginning of my trip only a few weeks ago and it feels like it was years ago.

Every night I have prayed that we do not need to come out - that is, that the Israeli army does not invade the village at night in order to arrest the people they can not arrest during the demonstrations due to the international presence. Every morning I have woken up in gratitude that we did not need to come out.

Today M. comes and shows us some great videos that explain, among other things, the history of the Palestinian rip-offs. Apparently it all started in an honest way when some foreign Jews began to legally buy land in the late nineteenth century. Then the Israeli government stole and conquered from the mid twentieth century. The potential Palestinian State, "granted" by the United Nations, got smaller and smaller and more and more fragmented, to the point that it is no longer viable, becoming what it is now: a few territories scattered apart and surrounded, besieged, each of them, by ... THE WALL.

Bi'lin is very near Ramallah; in fact the road that communicates with what is now the de-facto capital of Palestine is one of the very, very few, that I have seen here without a permanent military checkpoint. It is not a long road; it usually takes taxis fifteen or twenty minutes to arrive here depending on the amount of passengers they need to drop. It is because of this proximity to Ramallah that this small city is affected by the Wall that is being built around Ramallah. Again, Israel says it is for security reasons. Again too, deeds demonstrate that it is one more exercise, more or less civilised, of land theft.

Fig 10: Illegal settlement behind mountain

FIFTH WEEK

Fifth Monday - **Jews, Muslims and Christians**

M. takes me to the neighbouring village to buy some fruit today. He tells me a curious anecdote about this village: the church was very old and needed repairs, and the Muslims insisted on paying for half the cost. I observe that everyone dresses in the same style as in the rest of Palestine and I ask him where the Christians are.

"What do you mean?"

"The Christians. The women who do not need to cover their heads. Where are they? Everyone is dressed as a Muslim"

"Ah. No. The Christians wear the same."

"So covering their heads is not a religious thing, but a cultural custom." And I go on about how surprised I am by the fact that Christians and Muslims live together in the same village.

"Well, yes, and Jews too."

"You mean in some settlement."

"No, not in settlements. In the village."

"Jews in the occupied territories?"

"Yes."

"But, did they not throw them all out, the Romans?"

"Some managed to stay, never left. But the Israelis treat them the same as Palestinians. They are just Palestinians for them."

Fifth Tuesday - **The settlement-city**

At first sight, the Israeli settlement near Bi'Lin is not recognisable as such. It does not look like the other settlements we have seen at all. This one looks more like a horrible mega-city than a pretty little village. From where I am I can only see the bits that show beside the hill that conceals most of the city. The locals say that the city-settlement can house five thousand people. Fig 10

The land where this settlement-city stands used to belong to a local farmer. He used to own eighty square kilometres before the occupation; now the illegal seizures without compensation have left him with five.

Fifth Wednesday - **Tea and cakes**

W. and I go for a walk and we get lost. As we are figuring out our way back, we stop on a corner, trying to decide which way to go, then someone calls us from the doorstep of a nearby house. A woman is making gestures inviting us into her house. We look at each other and decide this must be just another sign of the great Palestinian hospitality.

She leads us into her house and, following her, we arrive at a little patio garden. There are two empty chairs as part of the circle where the family is sitting and they invite us to sit on them.

The woman who has brought us here disappears inside the house and we are left with two boys, a little girl and an older man. We assume he is the father.

It is the boys that lead the conversation. They tell us they are in university, and that they know there will be no jobs for them when they finish. The girl is still in school. She is more than looking at me, she has her eyes fixed on me. It is a bit uncomfortable but I understand that it must be quite unusual for her to see a woman my age with her head uncovered in the presence of men who are not part of her family. I ask her her name but she just smiles and looks at her brothers shyly.

The woman comes out to the garden and offers us tea, together with some cakes that look very similar to a kind sold in Ramallah. They confirm that the cakes are from there; the father brought them home as a special treat for the family. There is tea for every one, but the cakes are only for W. and me. They tell us that if we do not want them now we can take them home. We can not refuse and I decide then that they will be my special breakfast tomorrow.

Like other Palestinians we have met, they ask us about our lives at home, in our countries. They also want to know why, of all Palestine, we are in this little town. We say it is because of the Friday demonstrations and the night raids.

"Yes, but how did you find out?"

We try to explain the whole story, but his English is limited and our Arabic is non existent. So we shorten it:

"You know M.?"

"Yes."

"We are staying at his place. He is in a group, we came to that group. They say, 'we need people in Nablus, in Bi'Lin'. So we come".

He stares at the floor and I guess he would like to ask more but he just looks at us and says:

"Thank you."

And I do not know what to answer. We come into his house, we drink his tea, we take away the very few cakes that the father must have brought on a special trip, he walks us home and he still needs to say "Thank you".

Fifth Thursday - **Israelis against the wall**

Tomorrow is the weekly demonstration in Bi'Lin. Demonstrations here are never dull. They do not consist of just marching from point A to point B. From the used materials I have seen around from previous demonstrations, like banners and customs, it seems that they make creative props for every demonstration. We will probably march as well, but we know that there will be soldiers and that they will use violence and weapons of various kinds.

A few men and boys come to the flat to work on tomorrow's props. Some more internationals come, both Israelis and foreigners. H. has arrived from Jerusalem. He tells us that the army have forced their way into the hotel where I visited A., in East Jerusalem. Apparently the soldiers were looking for Palestinians who do not have permission to be in Jerusalem. They searched the whole hostel but thankfully nothing else happened. It could have been true that they were looking for some "illegal", or it could have been just a routine harassment exercise against a tourist hostel run by Palestinians.

The Israeli state has not only revoked the permit that thousands of Palestinians used to have to work in Israel. They also deny many Palestinians the right to "travel" to places like Jerusalem, and all the territories "officially" recognised as Israel. That includes the whole of Jerusalem, even though the "international community" still recognises East Jerusalem as part of the "Palestinian Territories" and the capital of the future Palestine. The Israeli policies have made this unfeasible and now Ramallah is the "de facto" capital.

When the prop-makers finish, they show us a few videos of previous demonstrations. We follow what goes on in the videos thanks to the subtitles. The Israeli soldiers never speak to the Palestinians in English in front of the cameras. When the tear gas makes its entrance, one Palestinian asks the soldiers to stop shooting tear gas and other chemical weapons at the peaceful demonstration. The Israeli soldier shouts in Hebrew what the subtitles translate as:

"Get rid of the foreigners first! Get the foreigners out!"

The videos finish and more Israeli activists begin to arrive to spend the night here and attend the demonstration tomorrow.

We all have some dinner sitting on the floor and I speak to the woman sitting next to me, an Israeli born in Sweden. She tells me that she learned Hebrew in six months, because it is very easy. Now she masters it, she says, and she is learning Arabic, which is much more difficult. She has been studying it for years and she can not have a fluent conversation yet. Besides, it is difficult to practise it, because the Palestinians want to practise their English, or show off that they can speak Hebrew. Almost all Palestinian men, she says, can speak Hebrew, either because they have worked for the Israelis, when it was allowed, or because they have been in jail. Not so much the women. That is why she likes to hang around with Palestinian women and children, to speak in Arabic with them.

Now that I think about it, I have not encountered any Palestinian who can not at least give me directions in English. It might be because I have been to places where they are used to seeing and talking to foreigners.

B. tells me how, as a Jew, she could come here with more rights than the Palestinians, and live in legal Israel or in one of the illegal settlements specially prepared for immigrants like her thanks to the land thefts. She has chosen to live in a more modest location and take every single Friday off to come and support this demonstration against the illegal wall - although, after a few weeks here, it is difficult to know what is legal and what is not.

She seems to know a bit about the wall and the people building it. She says it is Palestinians themselves, having been deprived of their land, their livelihood, and then the right to work in Israel. When they are offered work as builders of the wall, they truly are desperate enough to accept the job.

"There is not one single Israeli worker involved in the construction of the Wall. Just the soldiers guarding it. The Palestinians themselves are forced to build their own jail. The Israeli State is depriving the Palestinians of all dignity."

She also tells me stories of other demonstrations in other villages against the Wall, where there were not any internationals or Israeli activists. In one of those, the Israeli soldiers killed four Palestinian demonstrators. This, she tells me, never happens when there are foreigners present. So the mere presence of privileged foreigners seems to stop killings.

F. is French and something of an economist, or similar, from the way she speaks. She says she has talked about Palestinian agriculture with many Palestinian farmers and the conclusion is always the same: that Palestine has a lot of potential to be a rich Country, to develop from an excellent production, capacity and know-how. But the Israeli state stops it all.

I remember that in History lessons at school, it was explained that, when the Catholic King and Queen expelled the Jews and the Arabs from the kingdoms of Castilla and Aragon, they had to allow one Arab family out of ten to stay in the Levante region because they were the only ones who knew about farming. I can see that wisdom here too, in their irrigation systems, in how they keep their vegetable gardens in the conditions of deprivation imposed on them by the Israeli army... everything I have eaten here, especially in the villages, is the produce of their own land, and it is really excellent: the oil, the zahtar, the bread, the olives, the tangerines, the clementines ... but as F. says, what is the point of all this, if the occupation forces do not allow any of this produce out of the country!

F. continues to say that what has happened since the arrival of the Israeli State is a continuous strangulation of the Palestinian economy: first they take away their land and make its inhabitants refugees, then they take away their water, then they put those refugees and other destitutes to work for the occupying population, then they forbid this way of subsistence while they steal more land and more water; and all the while they do not allow any commerce with the outside world, or even with the occupying population. And then I remember a settler telling us that the only aspiration of the Arabs is to fly away from the country to make a fortune elsewhere.

Fifth Friday - **Gas, bullets and stones**

There is a demonstration against the wall every Friday in Bi'Lin. The wall here is just a metal fence next to a road attached to it, like the one we saw in Jayyous. It is called a wall because it is also used to separate communities and steal land all the same.

More Israeli and international activists arrive during the morning and the street is quite crowded, even before the Palestinians come out of the mosque. J. and A. are some of those internationals and we update each other on what we have been up to since we last saw each other. A. has been here, in Ramallah and Jerusalem, and J. has been in Hebron and Kawawis. I mention that it might be too late now for me to visit those two places, because I am leaving pretty soon. They say it is worth trying and they encourage me to go. I answer that if I leave, then Bi'Lin will be left without internationals, and it is when there are no internationals that the Army enters. Their argument is that I should make the most of this trip and see as much as possible in order to tell the tale back at home. He has a point. But have I not seen enough? And today I am going to see a demonstration...

"You have not seen Hebron."

B. strongly recommends us to get some perfume to counteract the smell of the tear gas. I go to the shop with her and I buy a bottle of water too because she also says that it is going to be a few hours fight, so it is better to have something to drink at least. The shop keeper knows what this is for and gives us a very special price.

At about noon, when the Palestinians come out of the mosque, there is a good few of us, between the Palestinians, Israelis and the rest. Israelis and foreigners have different "privileges": the soldiers are less likely to arrest or harm internationals; they are more likely to arrest or listen to Israelis. Privileges, the Palestinians have none. The soldiers are most likely to arrest and shoot at Palestinians. So, each with our different privileges, off we go to the demonstration all together.

Almost all of the Israeli activists are wearing Palestinian shawls. Some foreigners wear them too, but I did not bring mine here because I was told that if they saw it when searching my luggage at the airport it would have been a lot more difficult to be allowed into the country: if you are suspected of supporting the Palestinian cause, then you are a potential terrorist and you are not allowed to enter. And interrogations and searches are said to be even worse upon departure, so I have not even bothered to buy myself one.

When the demonstration gets near the wall, the soldiers simply block the way. For about half an hour all the Palestinians do is chant in Arabic and dance in front of the soldiers. The "shebab", the youngsters, look like they want to reach the fence, and the soldiers' job, in theory, is just to avoid that, to stop them.

Some of the "shebab" go down the hill in order to get to the fence across the field. The soldiers follow them and when the young Palestinians outnumber them, they throw tear gas at them. They can not use anything more than sound bombs and tear gas, while the Palestinians do not throw stones. When they do, the are legally allowed to use live ammunition. "Carte Blanche". That is why they provoke them, to get them to throw stones and then be able to shoot at them. For the moment they leave us internationals and Israelis alone, on the one hand because they know that we are not going to throw stones, and on the other because there is no "carte blanche" with internationals. For now.

According to what the Israelis tell us about the Army's rules, they can only throw tear gas in an ellipse, because the objective is not to harm people with the canister that contains the gas but just to disperse us. But now I see a soldier kneel and point his machine gun directly to the head of one of the Palestinian boys, almost kids, who are already retreating towards the village, across the field, away from the wall. I point my camera at him, and immediately another soldier pats on his shoulder and nods towards me. I see him move his lips and I read "filming". The one with the machine gun looks at me and stands up. My camera has just avoided one shot on a head. But it will not avoid all of them.

Someone in the crowd tells the soldiers, in English, that what they are doing breaks international law. One of the soldiers responds:

"International law does not apply here. Only Israeli law."

Action goes on around me and I have to stop staring and pointing with my camera to avoid the baton of a soldier and run. Suddenly we hear a shot and the sound of a tear gas canister being thrown to the air. The smoke trail is not elliptic; it goes in a straight line, right to where the kids are. They are not running any more, because they are picking one of them up, who has fallen down. Blood is coming out of his head. They have hit a Palestinian kid in the head with a gas canister. This is what they wanted.

The soldiers also want to gas us but they can not because we are too close to them, and if they do, it will affect them too. They need to make us go further away first. So it all consists of a continuous up and down the road up to the wall. The soldiers push us, shout at us, sometimes in English but more often in Hebrew, they hit us with batons, drag us, beat us with the back of their guns, pull our hair, until at some point we can not take it any more and we run away from their violence.

In the short moments when there is a few metres distance between the soldiers and the demonstrators, the soldiers run away from us to increase that distance and throw tear gas canisters at us. Then we run towards them to cut that distance again, so that they can not gas us, and it all starts all over again.

I ask when this will finish because I can not see the end and it feels eternal.

"It can go on like this for about two or three hours", says J. He has been here before. And I wonder if we will simply go back home, hurt and tired of this "game", or who on earth will decide when this will finish.

For the next two hours the dance up and down the road is repeated again and again and the air fills with tear gas, shootings and screams. We cover our faces with shawls or scarves; these and our cameras are our only weapons.

But we can not cover our eyes, and they hurt. And the tear gas is suffocating. And yet we are not in back streets or tunnels; we are in the open air and the gas disperses quicker than in urban demonstrations. Most of us, including J., A. and me, run so far away from the soldiers that we almost get back to the town, and some hide behind a house. I look back to check that J. is coming with us, I see him about five steps away from me and half a second later a gas canister passes between the two of us, leaving a straight smoke trace behind it, almost as swift as a bullet. (Feeeeeuuuuuuuuuuuuu!!) I scream in terror.

No one has been hit and the action continues. We all hide behind the house. My legs tremble. After a short time it all gets calmer and we all get out, back to the demonstration. I want to stay: it is too horrible and I am scared. J. shouts at me in Arabic:

"Ya-la!" (which is so similar to the Spanish "¡Hala!", and which translates as "come on"). I shout back:

"What do you mean, ya-la!" and the Palestinians laugh.

Slowly, feeling no urge whatsoever to get anywhere near the soldiers again, I walk behind the people who are already running towards them. And the show starts all over again.

During all these scuffles two Israelis have been arrested. However, since they have similar rights to those that westerners would have in their countries, it is not considered that their lives are in danger or that their families are at risk. But if a Palestinian is arrested, who knows what can happen to him. They can accuse him of whatever they want and, since he is not going to have the right to know what he is accused of, it is very likely that he will at least spend time in jail, and will be lucky to come out as healthy as he went in.

Suddenly some women come out of nowhere and everywhere and start yelling at the soldiers. That is how I learn that a Palestinian has been arrested. A. explains:

"There are never any Palestinian women in demonstrations" - and I realise that indeed the only women until now were Israelis and foreigners - "but when they arrest a Palestinian, their women come out and yell at the soldiers, that's what they do". It is the only thing they dare to do, but you can see all the rage and impotence in those yells, in how they look at the soldiers, and at us, especially one of them, older than the others. A. tells me that she is the mother of the arres-ted man.

There is not much we can do, apart from giving in to the Israeli soldiers' blackmail: "We release him once you have gone home". That is: the hostage in exchange for the end of the demonstration.

All the conversations and negotiations go on in Hebrew so I find out what is going on thanks to some Israelis who translate from time to time. The Palestinians are saying that the soldiers should release the hostage first and then we will go. The soldiers say we should go away first, away from the wall, and then they will release the hostage. People begin to leave bit by bit but the arrested man's mother stays and a few Palestinian women join her and sit down on stones by the side of the Palestinian "road" that is cut short by the wall we are protesting against, and which still continues on the other side, now completely useless. A few Israeli girls stay with them as well.

Bit by bit, the demonstration has split between men and women. The men are further away from the wall and the soldiers, while the women sit right next to them. I ask one of the Israeli girls if it would be ok to film the Palestinian wo-men. She tells me to ask them. I ask her to act as an interpreter and she agrees. She asks them and the hostage's mother answers:

"For many years we have been photographed, filmed, and it has changed nothing".

I sit down next to them, with my camera off, waiting, with them. The soldiers are standing, near us. Most of us are sitting down. They are not looking at us; they are looking at the men further down. It looks like they are expecting some-thing from them.

A Palestinian man comes, looking like he is going to speak to the soldiers, but he speaks to the mother of the arrested man. The woman is a lot older than the man speaking to her. She gets up, looks at the rest of us, says something brief and they all get up too. I follow. I ask an Israeli girl what is going on and she just tells me that the man is commanding us to join them, away from the soldiers.

"But the women wanted to sit down here..."

"Such is their culture. A man comes, tells them to go, and they go".

I join J. and A. and we just continue to wait.

A van comes down the road from the wall under construction, full of young Palestinian men who have not been in the demonstration. They stop and talk to the Palestinians waiting with us. I ask A.:

"Who are they?"

"They are scum."

I make a face of disapproval and he explains that they are the workers actually building the wall. They work for the Government of Israel and then they are treated just like any other potential terrorist, not allowed to use the roads they build, having to use others, like this one, cut off.

"OK, they are not scum", says A. "They work for them. They are building their own jail. They shouldn't..."

"They probably have no other choice if they don't want to starve."

After a good while the soldiers decide to release the hostage and there is great joy amongst us. Honouring the "agreement" with the soldiers, most people head home. A. and J. confirm that this is it for today.

Considering the demonstration finished, the three of us sit down on some rocks to have a rest. More workmen come from the wall, these ones on foot, and two of them come up to us to talk. They say they are from Hebron. They come here every day but still they have to use Palestinian roads and go through the checkpoints.

There are a few soldiers on the top of a hill made out of rubble now. They are looking at us, or maybe looking at some boys who have covered their faces and heads with Palestinian scarves and are now practising with some slings, without throwing stones. But after a few minutes they do start throwing stones at the soldiers.

I look at them and then I look at A.

"They should improve their aim", he says. I make a face and he continues: "Legitimately, they could defend their territory with guns. This army has invaded their country, this is an illegal occupation of a land that is legitimately theirs, and the only weapons they have are their stones".

"But throwing stones doesn't improve the situation."

"It's not for us to judge them. It is not our land, nor our country. It is their war, not ours."

He must have a point because I feel that whatever I answer, I will be judging them.

The boys throw stones but none of them falls anywhere near the soldiers on the top of the hill. The rest of the Israeli soldiers have disappeared into the armoured vehicles parked next to the wall. The rest of the demonstrators have also left. It is only the three of us left with the Palestinian boys from Hebron. They are very keen to see the pictures taken on our cameras.

The boys with the slings are about forty or fifty metres away from us, to our right. The soldiers are in front of both groups, on a strange lonely hill; maybe one or two hundred metres away straight ahead. To reach them, we would have to go down the bottom of a valley, which we can not see from where we are, and then up their hill. There is a mild breeze coming from our right. The boys go on throwing stones at the soldiers. The soldiers look on but they do not do anything. We know that anything can happen once the boys throw stones, that the soldiers have "carte blanche" to use whatever weapons they want. It is just as well if they want to shoot live ammunition. Our presence, or our cameras, may be what is stopping them from doing that.

The guy from Hebron sitting next to me asks me to show him my pictures and I show them to him one by one, discreetly looking at the soldiers at the same time. Then one of the soldiers throws a tear gas canister that falls between the guys with the slings and us. We can not see the canister but we can see the smoke, already familiar, coming in our direction, vanishing in front of us without enveloping us. We cover our noses out of habit but the smoke has cleared away from us.

The guys with the slings go away and leave us there in front of the soldiers, but the demonstration has finished a while back now, and now that there is no one throwing stones or gas canisters any more, we feel we can relax and stay here having a rest after running up and down. It is quiet all around us, so I concentrate on the pictures I am showing to the guy sitting next to me. He tells me that he comes here from Hebron every day to work for Israel building the wall, that he hates doing it but he needs a job to support his family, that there are no other jobs available and that he is not allowed to emigrate elsewhere to find work.

And then suddenly my throat begins to itch violently. I cough and my nose gets blocked and my eyes ache and cry when I blow my nose, and my whole face is in pain. And it is strange and terrifying because I can not see what can be causing this. It is coming without coming from anywhere.

I can hear the others cough too, but I can not see them. The pain does not let me open my eyes. Still I need to see my colleagues. I force myself to open my eyes, painfully, just enough to see the shape of J. and his bandanna covering his face. He seems to be walking towards the town.

During the demonstration, we were witnessing every single canister that was thrown at us, we could hear the blast first, then we would see the smoke, and then the smoke would dissipate leaving a strange smell behind.

But now we have not heard anything; we have not seen anything. We have not noticed any change in the air. And yet these strange and painful things are happening in my nose, my eyes and my mouth, and it looks like it is happening to the others too.

I have not felt this bad during the whole day, which is remarkable because we have indeed received gas today. But earlier today we could just run away from the smoke and that was it, I stopped smelling it, and I ran, and came back, and they would throw another canister, and back to the beginning. Now the air looks completely clean, yet we have just been violently stricken by these horrifying symptoms.

As soon as I can react I follow J. and A., running away from there, coming back home.

While I run almost blindingly, I remember. It is not the smoke that is the gas. The gas itself is invisible; you can not see it. The smoke tells you that the gas is coming, but the invisible gas spreads much faster and further away than the visible smoke. And, although you can breathe normally, it provokes who-knows-what chemical reaction in your brain that makes you feel that you can not breath, so you breathe more deeply, which makes you take even more gas into your lungs and more paranoia into your brain.

But this is even more brutal than that. We were not told about the throat itching and going dry and not being able to stop coughing and crying. We were not told about the panic or the pain either. This thing, which is now attacking our bodies, which is making every part of them, especially our faces, ache, and which we can not see, was not mentioned to us.

My eyes cry and ache. My nose is loaded as if I had a tremendous cold. And this dizziness... This is different from the tear gas we received before.

We get home and the symptoms ease little by little. I need to talk about what is happening, put it into words, verbalise it, put it into perspective, or my brain may burst.

"So these are the biological weapons. You can not see them or feel them, they simply destroy your insides, and you are still unable to see anything not normal, out of yourself or on your skin, but your throat burns and your eyes ache."

"This is it, they are using biological weapons against unarmed, peaceful demonstrators", answers J.

"But, why this last act? The demonstration had finished, we were having a rest, all had finished. Even the boys throwing the stones had left."

"The soldiers needed to get rid of us and our cameras before using live ammunition".

"With the direction of the wind, they knew that, throwing the gas where they did, it would come directly to us. That gas was directed at us from the moment they threw it, not to the stone throwers. The boys with the slings must have known this. That's why they left the moment they saw the smoke, because they knew that the gas would make us leave and the live ammunition would come next."

Fifth Saturday - **The day after the demonstration**

Imagine you live in constant tension. Imagine that there is nowhere safe where you live and you can never peacefully go to sleep. Imagine that tonight, as you are falling asleep, you hear someone knock on your door asking to enter. Imagine that the person you live with, your wife, your flatmate, your mother... gets up and opens the door for them. Imagine the person who enters is another person who lives with you; your son, your flatmate's girlfriend, your father... and imagine that now, knowing that everyone who lives in your house has finally come back home at the end of the day, only now can you know that all of your family has lived for just one more day.

Now imagine that the people who are knocking on the door are not people who live with you, but they are soldiers coming for you, or your wife, or your parents, or your children. Imagine you can never sleep in peace thinking that they can come at any moment. Imagine that every time someone rings the door bell, your whole family comes out to the living room terrified, looking into each other's eyes, deciding whether or not to open the door...

J. and A. left yesterday evening, with all the other Israeli and international activists who came just for the demonstration. A handful of us have stayed to "cover" for the possible incursions and raids.

It is dark at night when two of the people staying with us arrive and find the front door locked. They go all the way round the building until they find one light on: mine. They knock on my window and ask me to open the door for them. The door makes quite a lot of noise, even though I try to open it silently. We have not got back to our rooms yet when we see the upstairs neighbour coming down with an expression of panic on his face:

"Who made that noise?"

"Us."

"No one else?"

"No, no one else. We're just arriving now, we're sorry to bother you at this time."

"No bother. I thought they were soldiers."

Fifth Sunday - **Internet Relay Chat**

<friend> how's it going?

<friend> everything all right?

<me> yes!

<friend> cool :)

<me> I am in Bi'lin, a place where absolutely nothing happens during the day

<me> so no one wants to be here, because most people are big boys in need for action and adrenaline

<friend> ok

<friend> so you are staying in Bi'lin for a while

<friend> and do you like being there?

<me> well I like it because I don't like violence, nor tense situations

<friend> violence?

<me> yes, especially from the settlers

<me> I went to a demo the other day, with tear gas and bullets,

<me> what an adrenaline shot

<me> no wonder people get into these things so much

*<friend> f***ing hell*

<friend> watch out what you get into! :)

<me> well the bullets are rubber bullets

<me> in theory

<me> they are made of metal and then they have a very thin layer of rubber

*<friend> and they f***ing hurt*

<me> I was screaming like mad

<me> just from looking

<friend> watch out

<me> those are the bullets that happen in this village, every week

<me> and in those demos they don't arrest any one

<me> and if they arrest some one they use him as a hostage:

<me> we'll release him if you go home

<me> and they release him

<me> but then they do house raids in the night

<me> and they arrest kids out of their beds,

<me> and I've heard it is pretty violent

<me> that is why the internationals are here for the rest of the week

<me> but when there are internationals they do not make arrests in the night

<me> because they know that we record it and we put it on the internet

<me> so when we are here, it is boring

<me> you get it?

<friend> yes :)

SIXTH WEEK

Sixth Tuesday - **Last visit in Bi'Lin**

W. and I go out for a walk in the surroundings, observing the wall again and, as usual, we can not finish our walk without being invited for lunch. This time it is M. and his son inviting us to their roof terrace, to eat some olives. Communication is difficult so we only learn that all the land we can see on the other side of the wall/road belonged to M.'s father once.

While we are on the rooftop, we see a machine that I have never seen in my life before. We all look at it as it moves slowly over what looks like rubble from here. M. tells us:

"To take the olive trees."

I look at him in surprise and W. explains:

"That is the kind of machine they use to uproot the trees". Fig 11

Coming back home I decide that I am going to follow J. and A.'s advice and visit Hebron and Kawawis, to the South of Jerusalem. R. in Ramallah tells me that the checkpoint of Qalandia, between Ramallah and Jerusalem, is closed now, but surely in a few hours they will open it again. I ask him how long it will take me to get to Hebron and he says about two hours. In a normal country this would probably be about half an hour or an hour, depending on traffic, but here I will have to change taxis in Qalandia and then again in Jerusalem. W. and F. will stay here "on guard".

I have to be thankful that, in all the time I have been here, I have not had to come out one single night.

Sixth Wednesday - **The coffin-checkpoint in Hebron**

I come out of the flat where I have been staying since very early in the morning, careful not to wake up anyone. I do not want to risk arriving in Hebron after dark because I do not even know how to get to my destination, and this time, too, I am travelling on my own. The first stop will be of course Ramallah: first taxi change. From there, to Qalandia. R. assured me yesterday that I will pass through that checkpoint with no problem. From there I will get another taxi to Jerusalem and then another one from Jerusalem to Hebron.

But the taxi that takes us to Qalandia stops in the middle of a deserted road where there are only many taxis and a few people. In the distance we see a wire fence, cutting off what seems to be what is left of the road. The checkpoint is closed.

Facing that wire fence there are a very elderly man and a not-so-elderly woman. They seem to be standing there waiting for something. There are some small television crews around - two people per crew seem to be enough. Their cameras are tiny compared to the cameras available to students in some universities in London.

After filming a group of men who are reading a piece of paper stuck to the wall, written in Hebrew, one of the camera crews walks towards the couple. Me too.

The TV guys ask the man some questions and he answers and shows them some paperwork that he carries inside some envelopes. When he finishes talking and they switch off their camera, I ask the one with the microphone what is going

Fig 11: Machine to uproot trees

on. He tells me that the checkpoint is closed today because someone attacked a soldier yesterday, and that this old gentleman is very ill, that he has an appointment to go to the hospital and those papers are from his doctor and from the hospital, proving it all. He hopes to be allowed to go through on compassionate grounds. But it does not seem that he will be allowed at all. I ask the microphone man what will happen if he is not allowed to go through, if we are not allowed to go through.

"Turn around, go on another road."

"And how many hours will it take us to get to Jerusalem?" He moves his head, grins and answers:

"Hmmm... maybe two, three hours".

From Qalandia to the bus station in Jerusalem it usually takes about half an hour, sometimes less. But then I will still have the rest of my trip ahead, to Hebron. Two hours was all it was going to take me to get all the way to Hebron.

But the man does not lose hope and calls a soldier he sees in the distance to talk to him. The soldier comes, making sure another one comes with him, and both come slowly - they have the whole day and a lot of contempt. The soldiers coming towards us look just like all of them, with their green uniforms and their arms leaning on their huge machine-guns. For about five minutes the man talks to them and he shows them his papers, which they do not even touch or look at. He is trembling. His hands are trembling a lot, and he puts away his papers and he does not know where to put his hands, and he leans them on the barbed wire, and he cries in desperation at the thought that he will not make it to his appointment at the hospital, and he writhes in pain, and sits on the road... How is he going to start a two or three hour journey now, in his condition? He needs to go to hospital, can they not allow him to get through?

The soldiers' voices have grown more and more severe, and now they are almost shouting at him, and I can not believe my eyes and ears, even though I do not understand a word.

Suddenly the soldiers stop looking at the man who is writhing and they look at me, and then at something behind me, and they shout. I look behind me in the direction they are looking and I realise that more and more men have been approaching this spot and there are now about thirty men behind the first group that approached the wire. The soldiers make gestures with their hands telling them to go away, to retreat. Bit by bit they all go away, looking for taxis that will take them to Jerusalem. When all the men who were behind me have left and next to the wire there is only the trembling man, the woman, the TV crew and me left, the soldiers shout at me that I should leave too, and I leave. The woman that was with the trembling man leaves as well, and we leave him there, trembling and crying, while the TV crew seem to try to convince him that he is not going to manage to go through Qalandia, that he will have to go round the long way like the rest of us, or die right there.

Several taxi drivers ask me where I am going and I say I was going to get a taxi to Hebron in Jerusalem. They direct me to a taxi they say is not going to Hebron but is going nearby.

Once the taxi is full we depart and, after an hour into the journey, in a completely deserted road, we get a puncture. The driver asks us to get out so he can change the wheel and it turns out that the spare wheel is not in good enough condition. We all look at each other, but no one gets angry. The driver makes a few phone calls on his mobile and, after about half an hour, another van-taxi turns up to pick us up. Not a single car has passed by in all this time.

Like on all journeys where we share the means of transport, it is only when there is a setback that people talk to each other, whereas before we would not even look at each other. So our cultures are not that different in this respect.

The women talk among themselves in Arabic. One of them strikes up a conversation with me in English and she sets off to tell me her whole life. She is travelling with her son, who must be about six or seven years old, and they are going to Jerusalem, where her mother lives and where she was born. When she got married, she had to move to Ramallah, where her husband lived, among other reasons because he did not have - and does not have now - the necessary permit to "enter Israel", so he can not go to Jerusalem. So she has to travel on her own with her son to visit her mother, in taxis, and sometimes she has to spend the whole day travelling, like today, when they decide to close roads and make everyone go round on longer journeys.

We finally arrive at a place so full of people and cars that it looks like a market, but without stalls. There are militarily vehicles everywhere, and some soldiers on foot too.

The woman who has spoken to me grabs my hand and drags me along this taxi market, assuring me that she is going to find me one that will take me straight to Hebron from here. Some taxi drivers shout something that sounds like "Al Khalil" or "Al Halil" - which is how they say Hebron in Arabic. The woman tells me that the name of the city means "friend" both in Arabic and in Hebrew, then talks to a few of the taxi drivers and finally leaves me with one who, she assures me, will leave me very close to the address where I need to go.

The woman and I say goodbye and the taxi driver tells me to put my things at the back of the taxi and to get in too. I get inside but it is so hot it feels like an oven and I get out again. There is usually not a big difference in the number of women and men travelling, but today there are far fewer women. The man tells me for a second time to get in the car. I imagine it is not seen as correct for a woman to stand still, observing. I grab my camera and I use it as an excuse to stay outside. The men continue to look at me and the soldiers tell me with gestures: "No pictures".

When the taxi is finally full we set off, leaving the hubbub behind. About two hours later we arrive in the centre of Hebron. During that time we have seen many miles of concrete wall and gone through a couple of "flying" checkpoints, the ones that consist of three soldiers and a jeep parked across the road stopping the traffic. We do not need to get out at these checkpoints. The soldiers just look through the window and sometimes they do not even ask for our papers. Once in the centre of Hebron, what I have to look for is the checkpoint "inside" the city.

The taxi leaves us in a chaotic square full of yellow taxis, shops, people pulling carts full of fruit and vegetables, and noise. A "lot" of noise. This is the most noisy, lively and colourful place I have seen since I arrived in Palestine. People talk and shout, and the taxi drivers also shout and beep their horns at each other, arguing for the few inches of space they have available. The shops and market stalls, selling either clothes or food, expel bright, happy, shameless colours. The noise is deafening.

This part of Hebron, and the Old City, is in theory under the "rule of the Palestinian Authority". The part where the settlers live, where I am going, is under Israeli authority rule.

At the entrance of the streets that lead or are near the "Israeli section" there are some huge rocks to block wheel traffic. The stones are as high as my waist, and perfectly square and white. There are three or four in each street, leaving between them just enough space for one person on foot. Fig 12

In some cases, there are shops open in the rest of the street behind these rocks, but they are always fewer and smaller than on this side. Most of those streets are empty and silent, with all their green doors closed. Fig 13
Taxis are used to transport people. Most of them are small cars; there are hardly any vans. Wooden carts pulled by men are used for the transport of goods. It is the only way they can fit between the rocks.

Fig 12: Rocks in Hebron

The street I am looking for has those kind of rocks at the entrance too. All the shops on the other side of the big square stones are closed, showing only their closed green doors with stars of David painted on them. As soon as I go through these stones I get the feeling that I am entering a territory where I am not welcome. The street is, or seems, very short. It gets cut short by an iron structure that looks like a caravan, or a little prefabricated house, blocking the whole street from one side to the other. Whatever is on the other side can not be seen. The street is deserted, and that thing that is blocking the view is the checkpoint. There is nobody around. Fig 14

In order to get through this urban checkpoint I have to walk on some platforms that make a lot of noise. They are made of metal and they are not too well fixed to what I guess is the wood that keeps them elevated from the street. It feels as if they are suspended in the air, and they make a thundering noise with each step I take. Then there are two very high steps that someone elderly would find very difficult to climb. Then I have to open a metallic door and then climb up and get in at the same time.

This "caravan" is dark and claustrophobic inside, like a broken lift, or like a coffin. I can not see anyone. Behind me there is the door I have just opened, which closes behind me of its own accord. In front of me there is another door that will also need to open of its own accord, because it does not have a handle. So I am now trapped between these two doors that I can not open.

Fig 13: Street in Hebron

There is a kind of bad mirror to my left and suddenly someone shouts at me from behind it. I realise it is not a mirror, but smoked glass, and that there is a soldier on the other side looking at me and pointing at my backpack. I ask him if he speaks English and he orders me to open my bag with a hand gesture, without talking. I tell him it is only clothes. He makes yet another gesture ordering me to open my bag. I open it and I show him the top of it. He makes another gesture to get everything out of my bag, but there is no counter to put my things on it, so I have to kneel and get my things out one by one and put them on the floor, trying not to make them too dirty. Half way down my bag he looks like he is tired of it and he lets me know so, again with a gesture of his hand. I gather my things from the floor and I ask: "What now?" The soldier does not look at me but at least the second door gets open.

I get out into the sun again and I find a street similar to the previous one. In reality, it surely is the same one, only as it is cut short by this "thing", one can hardly realise. The atmosphere is completely different. There is a silence worse than sepulchral, like death, almost supernatural. In the distance, behind me, I can only hear the horns of the taxis, but they sound like a distant echo.

To my left there is another soldier looking at me from top to toe and in front of me I recognise D., whom I met in Nablus and who is now already coming to welcome me. I feel I could almost jump for joy, but the depressing atmosphere that invades everything is more powerful and we just shake hands smiling.

He tells me that he is patrolling the street, like I will be during the next week, while the kids are at school, but especially as they come and go. Part of the patrolling consists of observing this checkpoint, and that way we see everyone who comes and goes, and how long they detain each person. He also tells me that

Fig 14: "Checkpoint-coffin"

I can stay with him now if I want, but it is better if I go to the flat where we are staying to leave my things and receive some quick training at least.

For that I have to climb the steepest road I have ever seen, and then up to a fourth floor. There I meet K. and I see other people that I have met in other places. K. explains the geography and circumstances of this part of Hebron, and the neighbouring settlements that are making the life of their Palestinian neighbours hell. So much so that most Palestinian houses are empty. The only remaining inhabitants are people who really have nowhere to run away to and of course no possibility of selling their homes, because no one would want to buy them. And they do not resist. There are no demonstrations here, K. says, only silence, and an insane discretion, lest the settlers get angry. So taking pictures of them is out of the question, because they do not like it. Talking to them is out of the question too. It is too risky, they are too violent.

I ask K. about the checkpoint that looks like a coffin and he explains that it is unique in Palestine for now, but they will probably install more. He says that inside the cabin there are some electric radiations that are very bad for people in general, but for unborn children they are especially dangerous. There are many pregnant Palestinian women and everyone is worried, but of course this is not a worry for the Israeli authorities. Sometimes the pregnant women ask to be allowed to pass through a small corridor outside the coffin-checkpoint to avoid damaging their children but it all depends on how the soldier of the day feels.

In the street, up the steep hill, there are two "stations", or "posts", one on each side of the street, and with one or two soldiers each. And a bit further away, towards the left looking at the upper illegal settlement, there are another two. And right on the other side of them, further up, is the upper settlement, which in reality consists of about ten prefabricated houses planted in the middle of a street previously designated as an access road for the neighbouring Palestinians by some international treaty. Now this illegal settlement blocks the street and the only access is a muddy verge, which is also blocked by a barbed wire that can only be opened by the soldiers. K. explains that we are not supposed to go anywhere near there other than to challenge the soldiers when they do not allow Palestinians to go through the muddy verge.

K. is happy that I am staying here for a week. He explains that the worst days are Saturdays, the Jewish festivity, because the settlers take an especially sadistic delight in attacking the Palestinians on the Sabbath.

The street where I have met D. is very much a pass-through street, both for the children and teachers, to go to school, and for the settlers, to go from one illegal settlement to the other to visit each other. The Israeli settlers drive their cars on weekdays, and, as D. says, they drive like mad. It would seem they just want to kill every walking human being. Since Palestinians have no right to life in the settlers' minds, there is no reason to slow down if they see one crossing the street.

Palestinians are not allowed to use any vehicles in these streets. On Saturdays the Israeli settlers walk too, which is even more dangerous because a simple glance can infuriate them, and they have firearms. At least when they drive they do it too fast to aim and shoot.

I leave my things where it looks like I will sleep tonight and I help out in the "patrol", which simply consists of walking with the children at the end of the school day. Most of them are girls, because this school used to be a girls only school. When the children come out of school we go on "patrolling" until it gets dark, and then we go back home and we have dinner that we cook ourselves.

They tell me about the "women in black" and the "women in green". The Women in Black started as small support actions at checkpoints where Palestinians are retained for hours before they can continue their journeys. These women go and talk to the Palestinians in the queue, offer them tea, maybe some food too. The Women in Green turned up as a response, to support the Israeli soldiers, offering them the same in their posts around the illegally occupied territories.

I am invited to read a report of the most important "events" in the last few months. This is a small extract of this report:

"A group from the international Women in Black (i.e. Foreigners) came to Tel Rumeida with a small group of Palestinians. The group was near one of the settlements when they were stoned by a group of settlers, who used both stones and potatoes. Members of the Christian Peacemaker Teams (other foreigners) witnessed the violence from Qurtaba school.

"One of the Palestinian witnesses asked the soldiers who were watching the violence if they were going to do something, to which they replied, 'They're not Jews', implying that the safety of the internationals was not his concern.

"At 3:00 in the afternoon, children alerted us that settler children were stoning Palestinians at the top of the hill. When we (members of ISM, CPT, and the TR Project) arrived, we saw the five settler children, aged five to fifteen, inside the netted station of the captain. Such obviously biased behaviour is illegal and is a clear example of the type of obstacles Palestinians have to overcome when trying to assert their rights.

"We waited at the top of the hill and soon after, the settler children began throwing stones our direction, hitting a local 14-year-old Palestinian girl. We spent the next 10 minutes arguing with the soldiers to do something while the settler children taunted us and the Palestinians who were present. Finally, one soldier "reprimanded" the stone-thrower for five seconds, let him back into his station, and then sent the Palestinians and us out of the area. We all went to the top of the hill and waited for the arrival of the police.

"Five minutes later, two of the settler children left the soldier's station and walked up the hill to the settlement. On the way, they continued to throw stones at us. The soldiers near the settlement did not respond, so we again went to argue with them that something should be done about the settlers' vi-

olence. A captain immediately emerged, saying the area was a closed military zone and telling us to leave. During the ensuing argument, the settler children continued to throw stones, taunted us, and tried to take our cameras. One of the Palestinian children was hit on the arm by a stone and identified the stone-thrower, a boy about 14 years old.

"The police arrived more than 40 minutes after they were called, though they are stationed less than 2 kilometres away. They said that they could not arrest anyone younger than 12 and said that with these younger children, their only form of recourse is to speak with their parents about their children's behaviour.

"When two members of the TR (Tel Rumeida) Project were leaving, one of the soldiers on duty alternatively called us 'dirty pussies', made a joke about his penis, and yelled, 'you have big boobs'.

"At 7:30 in the evening, Palestinian children reported that two bikes and three carts were stolen from them by the settler children. Though soldiers were present and watching the incident, they did nothing. In fact, one of the children reported a soldier - the same Druze soldier who let the settler children in his station earlier that afternoon - only responded when the Palestinian child tried to stop the settler from taking his cart. At this, the soldier grabbed the Palestinian child by the neck, letting the settler take his cart.

"When we arrived, the Palestinian boys were sitting in the street waiting for the police to arrive. While waiting, a settler woman arrived. We recognized her as Miriam Levinger, the co-founder of Kiryat Arba, the first settlement in the West Bank. The first words out of her mouth were, 'Do you deny that I am a descendent of Abraham?' The conversation continued along much of the same vein, with Miriam yelling at us, calling us anti-semites, and talking about Muslim terrorism. The encounter ended with Miriam screaming in Arabic, 'Your father's a donkey, you're a donkey, your mother's a donkey...!'

"The police finally arrived more than 30 minutes after we arrived and told the children to be in the street the following morning at 8:30 and they would return their bikes and carts.

"A community leader went with the police to make a complaint and waited more than five hours at the police station.

"[The following day]

"The police were not in the street as promised.

"A community leader [and three internationals] went to the Kiryat Arba police station with four of the boys who had their carts and bikes stolen. The boys were 11 to 14 years old. Though the children had an appointment at 2:00pm with an investigator named Amitay, we waited outside the back gate for more than an hour. We all made multiple phone calls into the police compound, using the phone at the back gate and the main police phone number. The police inside the compound alternatively promised to open the gate, hung up, refused to answer, yelled, laughed, and taunted us.

"Finally, Amitay arrived at 3:15 and refused to let the internationals inside. After some arguing, he agreed that one could accompany the boys. However, he refused to let all four boys enter. The three who had their carts stolen were allowed to enter, but the one whose bike was stolen was not allowed in. I went inside with the kids.

"Once inside, Amitay explained that he was late because he had gone to Tel Rumeida to take the statement of various soldiers concerning the robbery and while there, the settlers punctured the tires to his police vehicle. This is the second incident of Tel Rumeida residents attacking police vehicles in less than a week.

"The boys began making their testimony at 3:45. Amitay refused to take the photographs of one of the settlers who was involved in the robbery and did not allow the boys to identify the settlers from police photos. He also yelled at the kids and made them wait to leave more than five minutes while he pretended to get the key and instead chatted with his friends. When I entered the room and stood staring at him, he yelled,

"My first mistake was letting you come in here!" I told him to just get the key and let us out.

"The kids were exhausted by the event."

I read these and more "events" in the document that K. lends me. I reach a point where I need to stop, unable to swallow any more humiliations. I stay there gazing into space until K. asks:

"What do you think of that?"

I do not find an English word to describe what I feel. I have to think of a Spanish one and then translate:

"Sickening."

"Yes, that's a good word to describe it."

Sixth Thursday - **The function of the human rights observer**

The neighbourhood where we are in Hebron, between two illegal Israeli settlements, is brutally depressing. It is one of those experiences where you think you are losing your sanity. We are in a Palestinian neighbourhood, between two settlements full of quite fanatic and fearful Israeli settlers. They are so fearful they routinely stone Palestinians and go out into the street with sub-machine guns. Fig 15

The function of the human rights observer here is to absorb the violence. Literally. Simply, to put ourselves between the Palestinians and the stones, as dialogue with these fanatics is absolutely impossible. They shout at us and they call us Nazis, because for them helping Palestinians is the same as supporting terrorists, because for them all Palestinians are terrorists and, according to them, if we help the Palestinians we do it because we hate the Jews.

This is the "conversation" we had with the Israeli settlers who deigned to talk to us today. Our cameras, acting as witnesses, annoy them big time, and we try not to make them angry. We make sure that we see the Palestinians go up the steps opposite the settlement safely, but we observe from a distance, trying not to provoke them with our presence. The presence of international observers stops the stonings from happening daily.

Fig 15: Settler with gun

Sixth Friday - **Anticipating the Sabbath**

Tomorrow is Saturday. As part of the Sabbath prohibition of any kind of work, strict Jews do not drive. Being as it is the Jewish weekly festivity, the street fills with settlers going from one illegal settlement to the other, carrying cakes in their hands and machine guns on their backs, in a kind of procession, all wearing black trousers, white shirts, black hats, beards and ringlets. Since they are walking, not driving, through the so hated Palestinians' neighbourhood, and walking takes a lot longer than driving, they also have that much longer to harass and terrorise the Palestinians. For a whole day every week, the Palestinians run the risk of being the victims of armed Israelis walking on the street.

The result is that Palestinians have learnt to fear Saturdays in this neighbourhood, and they do their best to spend the day elsewhere or locked in their houses. Indeed, all Palestinians here have done their best to spend the rest of their lives elsewhere. The remaining ones are only here because they really have nowhere else to go.

In the international flat we are already changing our daily plans for tomorrow: we will all be more alert and breaks will be shorter. Those groups that can afford it send more people to the streets as "reinforcements". Groups that can not, like ours, will just try their best not to send anyone anywhere on their own.

Sixth Saturday - **Kristallnacht**

In terms of "dangerousness", the Israeli children settlers are by far the most dangerous section of the population, more so than the adult settlers, who themselves are more dangerous than the soldiers. The reason for this is the criminal impunity the Israeli children enjoy. An Israeli minor does not have criminal responsibility; they can not even be arrested.

I am "on patrol" in the lower street of the neighbourhood, between the coffin-checkpoint and the steps that lead to the Palestinian school and homes, when the settler kids leave the school-nursery that is just at the bottom of the steps. I notice that some settler children are throwing stones towards the steps. They seem to be shouting at the steps and I understand they are either stoning some Palestinian, or just playing, or both. When they realise I am approaching them with my camera they change their target. As soon as they see me they start to scream at me and throw stones at me - about five stones, the size of a thumb. I start to film them but shortly into the recording my tape runs out. While they stone me, the woman they have been stoning so far just runs away back to her home. She probably will have to arrange for her family to eat somewhere else, if she can not do her daily shopping because of this. At least she has not been stoned - much.

I look at the soldier at the outpost that is opposite the steps, who has seen it all, but now he is talking on the phone. When he finishes I ask him:

"What are you doing about this? They are throwing stones at me", but he does not even look at me. His only function is to defend the Israelis from the Palestinians. It is not his job to defend the victims of Israelis.

There is no one else coming down the steps or approaching them from the street, so I just leave the scene.

At the end of the shift D. says that he can not believe that this has been a Saturday, because only my stoning and another two have happened today. Compared with any other Saturday, today has been extremely quiet.

I ask K. about the missing street lights. He explains the street lamps have been twice vandalised. In the Camp David agreements it was established that these Palestinian shops should be open so that the street would be as lively as the rest of Hebron. Then the Israeli settlers smashed the street lamps in a Sabbath vandalism orgy and when the workers came to repair them, the settlers stoned both the workers and the repaired lamps. The workers did not want to keep being stoned and they left, leaving the lamps vandalised, and there they remain, smashed. K. says that virtually each Saturday in this street is a "Kristallnacht", a Night of Broken Glass, with settlers walking down the street and smashing as much Palestinian property as they can. This was not one of those Saturdays and I am thankful.

Sixth Sunday - **Drug dealing**

Every day before breakfast we have the "morning shift". We go out to the street and, alongside other "international human rights observers", we stand at the sides of the streets that Palestinians need to use and which are closest to the illegal Israeli settlements. When the children are inside the school, other internationals stay patrolling outside it and we go up to our flat and have breakfast. After breakfast we go out again, and do the longer shift, until school finishes.

Today I leave this spot when the children come out of school and go up the hill, next to the other illegal Israeli settlement. Roughly half way between the two settlements that surround this Palestinian neighbourhood, there are two "outposts" for soldiers, one at each side of the street. In one of those outposts two soldiers are detaining a boy, for no apparent reason. They ask him for his identity card and I see them like playing with it, passing it to each other.

Our norm is to approach the soldiers after ten minutes to ask about the reason for the detention. A Palestinian boy approaches them and they ignore him. The instant I approach them, the scene changes. One of the soldiers takes the detained guy inside the tent while the other soldier keeps the Palestinian boy and me entertained in conversation. When we demand an explanation as to why the guy is being detained for longer than the army stipulates that someone can be detained before being arrested, the soldier that was chatting with us turns his back on us.

The Palestinian boy who approached them before me explains, in a low voice to avoid being heard by the soldiers:

"The soldiers are accusing him of drug dealing, and they are searching him, but he says he is not carrying anything, and he is not, because otherwise they would have arrested him already. Then they took his ID card and told him that unless he comes back within half an hour with cocaine they will not give him his ID back and they will arrest him for not carrying it with him."

I look at him in terror. He shrugs and says:

"Usual stuff".

My presence seems to grow too uncomfortable for the soldiers and they eventually let the boy go.

Everyone has to go through the coffin-checkpoint I went through on my arrival, every day, every time they need to go to the rest of the city, to go to work, to do their shopping, to go to school. And back. Of course people avoid it as much as they can. Everyone who could afford to move out left long ago. That is why the street is so deserted, lonely, sad, silent and dead.

Our day finishes at dusk, when no Palestinian dares to go out to the street. When something happens, they know where to find us.

R. comes to visit and tells us what happened to him today at the checkpoint. He was carrying his laptop computer. The soldiers made him open it. He opened it.

"Completely" said he soldier, making a move with his hand as if he was handling a screwdriver.

"I don't have a screwdriver here, I have one at home but it takes me half an hour to get there", said R. The Israeli soldier shrugged his shoulders. So there he went for a screwdriver, otherwise he would have lost his computer. And he had to open all the different components. The guarantee is no longer valid as a result, but the soldier will even say that he is lucky he still has his laptop.

SEVENTH WEEK

Seventh Monday - **Lies**

My favourite spot to patrol from is the place where I first saw D. when I first arrived here. The spot is good because from here we see, at the same time, the coffin-checkpoint to our right, and part of the illegal Israeli settlement to our left.

We are on a street used by the Palestinians to get to the school, which is just above the settlement, on a hill. The street is also used by Palestinians who live near the school to go to work, to other schools, or to the shops, as all the shops are closed in this neighbourhood. And it is also used by the settlers to drive (or, on Saturdays, to walk) from one settlement to the other, and to beat, stone ... and generally harass the Palestinians and make their lives unbearable since, in their opinion, they are no better than animals, scoundrels invading illegitimately the land that God bequeathed them.

The street is completely deserted because the Israeli government will not allow the shops to open. The international treaties signed by, among others, USA, Israel and the Palestinian authority, establish that all these shops should be allowed to be open. They actually established that they should all have been opened within six months of the date of the treaty.

D. tells me that every six months since then, a soldier goes to the end of the street, next to the coffin-checkpoint, and puts a piece of paper under a stone. On that paper it always says, in Hebrew only, that the shops will remain closed for another six months. So, years after the "treaty", the shops remind closed, and the treaty violated.

A young couple, made up of an Israeli soldier and a settler girl, comes along the street. They are holding hands but as soon as they see us they separate. D. tells me that the Israeli government always denies all links between settlers and soldiers, and what we have just seen is one more example of this lie. Fig 16

He then tells me that they routinely see settlers speak with the soldiers as if they were acquaintances, and that sometimes they have seen soldiers let settlers "play" with their guns pointing at Palestinians and making jokes.

Seventh Tuesday - **Apartheid**

It is mostly quiet in the street where I patrol. The street is usually deserted, apart from the soldiers and the odd Palestinian. The shops are all closed down. Their doors are all green but rotten because they are not used or looked after. Most of them have the star of David painted on them, just like the Nazis used to put signs on Jews' shops. Now it is Palestinian shops that have a Jewish sign on their doors. Fig 17

The only noise that breaks the silence within the area that is officially under Israeli control, is that of the settlers' cars. In the area controlled by Israel, Palestinians are not allowed to travel by car, or any other motorised vehicle. I have seen a couple of bikes around, but I have never seen them taken through the checkpoint. Israelis are allowed to drive any vehicle they want.

The consequences that these differences of rights have on their daily lives are quite painful, even seen from the comfort of the stone where I am sitting down, witnessing. We do not know how the settlers do their shopping as we only see them in their cars or when they take leisure walks, but we have seen Palestinians carrying heavy loads on carts and on foot, slowly, all along the street. Tasks that could easily take a fraction of the time and effort. But they have to be made arduous by the will of a power that has decided that a specific section of the population can only go around on foot or on a donkey.

Fig 16: Settler and soldier

Whilst Israeli settlers go about their daily lives protected in their cars and carrying weapons, the Palestinians are forbidden any kind of weapons and made to walk among these armed people.

Children from the illegal Israeli settlement go to their school in a van that makes several trips a day. Palestinian children walk to and from school only protected by the international presence that we foreign volunteers provide, armed with just our cameras.

A street-sweeping vehicle similar to those that we can see in European cities sweeping the streets cleans the streets inhabited by Israeli settlers. As Palestinians are not allowed to drive any vehicle, the street inhabited by Palestinians has to be swept on foot, with a broom. So there the Palestinian sweeper goes, with his bin in a small cart that he has to push, sweeping the street bit by bit.

The sweeper disappears around the corner towards the hill and then two Palestinian men emerge from the coffin-checkpoint. They are carrying a big sack that the soldiers make them open in order to inspect it. I can not see the content from here but it looks very heavy. The kind of load you would carry in a car, or at least a cart. But carts are not allowed through that coffin-checkpoint.

When the soldier lets them go, the men continue along the street, in front of me. One walks backwards, facing the sack and his friend. Every four or five steps, they stop, put the sack down on the pavement for a few seconds, and then start walking again. They smile at me and continue with their sack, stopping, resting and walking, stopping, resting and walking, slowly, towards the stairs at the other end of the street. Finally they go up the steps and I can no longer see them.

There are two skips, full of rubbish, opposite the checkpoint. One skip is for the Israeli rubbish; the other one is for Palestinian rubbish. Both of them are on a Palestinian street. It seems that the Israeli settlers consider themselves too pure to keep their rubbish container in their own street.

A huge lorry with Israeli plates brings rubbish and throws it into the Israeli skip. The lorry is driven by a Palestinian - they can not drive their own vehicles, but they can drive Israeli vehicles in order to provide services for the Israelis. The Palestinian skip can not be filled by a lorry, since the Palestinians can not drive motorised vehicles here. So the Palestinians have to manage the Israeli rubbish with Israeli lorries, but their own by hand.

Seventh Wednesday - "GAS THE ARABS!"

I am usually in the lower street, and I spend my hours watching in case that, in the distance, in the Israeli settlement, the Israeli settlers attack the Palestinian children when they go to school. But I have not seen the school itself yet.

The people who usually spend the whole day next to the school door to avoid attacks encourage me to go with them today so I can see the path the children need to walk to get there, and the school too. I go with them to the end of the street, the spot where we must not stay any longer than a few seconds or it will be seen as a provocation, and we set to climb the steps. But they are only steps by name. What I see is rather a rough hill full of random and broken stones. There are remains of what must have been a handrail, scattered all over the place. We finish climbing this hill full of broken stones that obviously used to be well sculpted thanks to some corners still intact, and the hill becomes a soil path bordered by trees. At the end of the path there are two small buildings. The one on the left is the school and the one on the right looks disused and has its door closed. There is a piece of graffiti on the door: "GAS THE ARABS! JDL". That, next to the school, is what the Palestinian children have to read every day.

I go back to my usual place and when the children come out of the school I go up the hill to be on guard. After dinner, the children enjoy themselves playing ball games or asking us to take pictures of them. If you take one's picture, you are done, they will not stop bugging you until you have taken two pictures of each of them, and then again in groups.

They spend most of the time after school in the street playing football - boys mainly; I see very few girls. Saving some differences, they remind me of my own childhood, when the street was our playground. I look at these children seeing myself in them. At least they have this space, like I did, before the cars invaded the street and evicted the kids of the next generations.

I say to A. that of course these Palestinian children are not in paradise, and surely they are maturing in a rush and they will not need to wait to be too grown up to understand the situation, but at least now they are having a better childhood than the kids in modern European cities, or even the kids in the local illegal settlements. I never see the settler kids playing in the street, only throwing stones, only doing acts of hatred.

"They are all terrorists"

I leave the street and the children in it for a moment, playing football, and when I come back, only a few minutes later, I find them sitting on the stairs next to the only open shop in the whole neighbourhood, because the soldiers have stolen their ball.

When I ask the soldiers why, they just look at me and keep silent. They have the power. Full stop. They have absolutely no obligation to speak to me. Another international comes and tells me that this is not the first time they have stolen the boys' ball. She asks them why they insist on making these children's lives impossible. One of the soldiers says:

"Because they're all terrorists."

My colleague tries to reason with them, saying that they are only children. The soldier mumbles and we hear him:

"Well, if they are not, their brothers are."

I can not believe what I hear and ask him to repeat it, but he remains silent.

I ask the kids about the details of what has happened. One of them, bigger than the rest, wants to stop them talking to me because I do not speak Arabic - I do catch that word. But the others confront him, they make him shut up and they answer my questions.

Fig 17: Green doors

They tell me that one of the soldiers simply grabbed the ball, and that this is by no means infrequent, although there is no rule that forbids them from playing. They tell me that some soldiers do not say or do anything when they are playing; it depends on what soldiers there are, each one acts differently, even each day the same soldiers act differently. One of the kids says that sometimes, the soldiers even play with them.

I guess that is what you do when you have absolute power over people who do not have any authority to turn to, who are absolutely unprotected, helpless.

The kids remain next to the shop until dark, when they all go home to their families. Later in the night I hear that the soldiers have returned their ball on condition that they will not play with it again.

Seventh Thursday - **The Israeli settler woman**

I am in the upper part of the neighbourhood today. An old woman from one of the illegal settlements walks up the hill, shouting at everyone she finds on her way.

I am told to be careful with her, although she is not usually physically violent. It seems she is one of those people who does not want people who are not Jews to be allowed to live on this land, and therefore it is necessary to make them disappear. She might be one of those who feel frustrated because they can not just do to the Arabs the same as the Nazis did to the Jews.

One of us, C., is walking down the hill when the woman stops to shout at her. After a few minutes of listening, C. continues walking down the hill to the street below.

Without stopping shouting, the old woman turns to us as she comes up the hill, then she sees me and starts to shout at me. After a few steps, she is finally close enough for me to distinguish what she is saying:

"You! Are helping the people! Who are destroying your civilisation! First they destroy Iran, then America! Now! Your turn!"

One of the other internationals tells me that this woman called him "German" once, with an insulting tone:

"She probably meant to say 'Nazi'", he explains, "because for many Jews, it's the same, but I didn't think at the time, I only said, 'No ma'am, I'm not German, I'm Swedish', and she replied: 'I'm sure you are related in some way with the Germans'".

The silence

There is a feeling of being in a cemetery here, really, it is so silent. The only constant sounds I can hear are of tooting horns, and they are very distant, as if coming from a dream. If that part of Hebron had not been the first thing that I saw of the city, I would still be wondering where those distant tootings were coming from. I imagine the settlers must be wondering that too because, according to D., they are not allowed to visit the "Arab" zone of Hebron, and in fact I have never seen a single settler in the nice part of Hebron.

Every night I go to bed begging that the following day will be at least as violence-free as the day just gone, still hearing the tooting horns in the distance, as if it was a dream already, and remembering how nice the city is on the other side of the coffin-checkpoint. The noise from the nice part of Hebron feels very, very far away from the middle of this silence of oppression and suffocation, and I go to sleep trying to imagine what these settlers would feel if they could witness how beautiful, multicoloured and happy life can be without them.

Seventh Friday - **The donkey**

Today D. and I patrol the lower street together, between the steps and the coffin-checkpoint. From here we see a man who is coming on a donkey to the part controlled by Israel from the part of Hebron that is still alive. I have seen him before. He does the same errand every day, and he is made to go through the same process every day.

I get closer to the checkpoint in order to video the whole "operation". Before entering the coffin, he has to get off the donkey and unload it, sack by sack, about ten sacks in total. They look quite heavy. Then he has to show the contents of each sack to the soldiers. Then he has to carry each sack to the other side of the coffin on his back. After this, he goes back to the other side and brings the donkey. He then puts every sack back on the donkey's back, as they were, and finally he gets on top of all the sacks to continue his journey. The operation has taken between ten and fifteen minutes.

He notices me as he goes up the hill on his donkey, or maybe he has noticed me recording the whole time. He looks at me and smiles, and I say thank you because it looks like he does not disapprove of my recording, although I have not asked him for permission. He also says "thank you". I respond "thank YOU", but he does not seem to understand and he thanks me again. Finally, he leaves.

J. emerges from the coffin-checkpoint at mid afternoon. I had not seen him since the demonstration in Bi'Lin, when he encouraged me to come here.

After updating each other about our latest doings and adventures, J. tells us about his doubts about what to do next. His idea for this trip was to go to Egypt after leaving Palestine and before going back to his country, because he has wanted to see the pyramids ever since his childhood. But now that he is here, and even knowing that most probably he will never have the opportunity to travel to the Middle East again, he is thinking of not going, and staying in Jerusalem instead. He wants to spend what he calls "quality time" with his friends; he does not want to travel through "normal" Israeli territory and the Egyptian desert on his own after this almost traumatic experience in Palestine, as if it had never happened, as if he could just walk around like a normal tourist now.

Yet he is worried that once at home he will regret having missed his only opportunity to visit the pyramids that he has so much wanted to see all his life.

We more or less agree that the ideal thing is usually to pay attention to one's feelings and do whatever one feels like as much as possible, and that it would probably not make much sense to travel to Egypt and risk being bitter, thinking how comfortable he would be in Jerusalem with his people.

For now J. is only passing on his way to Kawawis, which they say is not far away. He will stay there for just two or three days because there are no washing facilities there at all; then he will go back to Jerusalem. He recommends me to go to Kawawis too.

Seventh Saturday - **"You scummy piece of shit"**

There is a "visit" from the "Women In Green" (WIG) scheduled for today. It does not happen every Saturday, but they do come rather regularly. People who have been in Hebron for months are familiar with their doings.

K. and D. explain what the WIG normally do and what other human rights observers, people like us, have done in response in the past. The WIG usually go in a procession from Tel Rumedia, the settlement up the hill, to the other settlement below, the one just below the school where we watch that the settler kids do not throw (too many) stones at the Palestinian children and mothers. They try to schedule this "march" to arrive at the bottom of the steps right when the Palestinian children come out of school, and simply yell abuse at them.

On previous occasions, the internationals have usually tried to "escort" them in this march without provoking them, which is quite difficult because our mere presence is a provocation, so we should expect some abuse too.

Once they arrive at the bottom of the steps facing the coming kids, we need to place ourselves between the Women in Green and the kids. It is important that we do not face the children, but the women. This is to avoid intimidating the children even more. We need to face the women; they are the cause of the violent situation and it is them we should focus on, not on the children.

With these instructions we go out to the street prepared at least for the unpleasant.

We meet the WIG next to the coffin-checkpoint, where one can go either towards the lower settlement (or to my "watch point", in my case) or up the hill to the other settlement.

There is a boy being detained at the checkpoint and one of the internationals enquires why. As usual, there is no answer from the soldier. But there is another soldier who seems to be of some higher rank than the first one and he asks the international, a French woman, what her problem is. She starts:

"This soldier is detaining this boy..." At this point one of the women in green bursts out laughing:

"She's telling him the soldier is detaining 'that'! As if he cared!"

I start walking with the women in green (WIG) up the hill and the first girls coming out from school reach us. We place ourselves between the WIG and the girls. All the WIG take pictures of us, some with mobile phones, others with disposable cameras. There are also two men with them. They do not have cameras; they just walk and look at us in disgust. Most of the women with cameras have already taken a picture of me by the time we reach halfway up the hill. I take a picture of one of them, and one of the men says to me:

"Don't you have anything better to do, you scummy piece of shit?"

I look at him and see a pistol on his belt. As we walk up I place myself between this group and the children going up the hill too, to protect them.

They continue to walk to the settlement up the hill and, as they enter it, we leave them. They are not our business any more. Most of the school girls are now "safe" in inhabited Palestinian streets too.

But right on my left there is the muddy path through which Palestinian people are not allowed to pass to go to their homes, even though there is an international agreement and an Israeli court ruling that say they do have the right to pass. A Palestinian school girl is standing there hoping for the soldiers to open a bit of the razor wire that blocks the path for her. A soldier is standing there refusing to openm it. Two internationals are trying to reason with the soldier, which is usually useless, but today it seems especially frustrating. The girl gives up and walks down the hill, prepared to go all the way round hills and paths taking a good twenty minutes, to go to a house that I can see from here.

I start taking pictures of the path and the razor wire. I finish and we all start to walk down the hill, but a soldier starts pushing M. down the hill, saying that we have to go. M. falls on me and I am knocked down by the push too. I shout out and ask why. The soldier just says:

"You have to go."

I repeat:

"Why."

S. also asks why, but we get no answer; we are just pushed violently down the hill.

I then use my mobile to call D. to tell him about the situation. He asks whether the girl is being allowed through the path and I tell him that she gave up, so he tells me that we should walk down. We walk down but the soldiers still push us down violently.

I try to film them as they push us and, all of a sudden, one of the soldiers grabs my camera and pulls away, to steal it from me. I panic and start screaming. I have the strap of my camera tied to my wrist so my camera does not go. He does not let go, either, and he continues to pull and I scream, and scream, while I squat down on the ground, hoping that this will prevent him from taking my camera and arrest me. We struggle for a few seconds and he bends my glasses with his body, then my glasses fly off and I can no longer see them. He lets go of the camera but I continue screaming, asking for my glasses, panicking that I will not find them. Suddenly I see them under my foot - they are completely unusable now.

One of the women in green comes forward to me and, laughing, she screams:

"That was a very nice show, you are good for theatre!" She shouts other "funny" phrases, maybe even abuse, but she is the last thing that worries me right now, and, besides, I can not see her properly without my glasses, I can only see her shape.

Looking at my glasses, trying to figure out if they are fixable, we walk down the hill, towards our apartment, being pushed again by the soldiers. Far away, S. has filmed the whole scene. As we walk, another soldier quickly tries to grab my camera but I am faster and he can not even touch it. I then see S. being pushed around: some soldiers are also trying to get his camera. I start filming again. Another soldier gets right in front of me and for a few seconds there is a cat and mouse game between the two of us, me trying to film the soldiers pushing S. around, and this soldier trying to block my vision. Looking at S. and this soldier in turns, I can not even see what I am recording. The soldiers have thrown S. to the ground and there he is, under a swarm of soldiers, lying on the ground, his belly down, his face up trying to look at me. It looks to me like they are arresting him. Between not seeing well without my glasses and the soldier playing games in front of me, I can only catch - badly - the moment when he stands up and is taken away - or so I think.

Usually it is S. or D. who call IDF (Israeli Defence Forces), and the rest of us just let them take care of the situation. But now S. is being arrested and D. is not here (where is he?). I call him to tell him that S. has been arrested and, at that very moment, S. appears round the corner, so I hung up. S. has not been arrested then, but he does not have his camera with him any more. The soldiers have stolen it. I am still shaking from the confrontation, and still looking at my glasses in despair. Some Palestinians have come out of their houses, probably alerted by the so unusual noise.

We try to regroup but in the meantime the soldiers have come in formation in front of us and they are already surrounding us. Suddenly eight or nine soldiers approach me and surround me and I do not see my friends any more. All I can see around me is green military uniforms, worn by big men with unfriendly faces:

"Give me the camera."

"No."

"You don't want to give me your camera?"

"Why do I have to".

Suddenly both of my hands are grabbed and my arms are spread wide by lots of hands. I scream with all my strength. Grabbing my left hand there are two soldiers. I only have my broken glasses in it. The rest of the soldiers, about six or seven of them, concentrate on my right hand, where my camera is. My body bends down as I scream and scream, and my thoughts go: "This is it, I am getting arrested, then deported, and then never again allowed back in Palestine, I got this far, it's over".

I go on screaming and still have my camera wrapped around my wrist so it will not go. The soldiers just twist my hand and my fingers, as much as they can, and they just pull the camera trying to rip off the strap, but the only thing that gets ripped off is my skin. I scream and scream fearing that they will break some part of my body or that they will arrest me. As I scream with my mouth open, I notice one of their arms firmly pressed against my mouth - how easy to simply bite this arm. But I understand that this is a provocation, because if I bite a soldier then they will have a reason to arrest me: "Assault to a soldier". But they do not seem to be arresting me, otherwise they would be dragging me to their vehicle by now, and they are not doing that, they are only struggling to get my camera. So, I just go on screaming, it is the only thing I feel I can do, given the circumstances.

Finally my thoughts go on to realise that I am only one and will not win against eight or nine soldiers, so I have to let the camera go, and at least stop them tearing all the skin off my hand. What is clear is that I will not prevent the theft of my camera, that is for sure.

When the soldiers finally get my camera they leave me there, shaking violently. A Palestinian woman then touches my shoulder and shows me a glass of water that she has in her hand. She then literally pours it inside my mouth - so much for lack of communication. I drink a bit and say "shukran" but she insists that I drink more, and I do. After drinking this water I am still shaking, although not so violently. Then I look around me and see that the street is full of people looking towards the group where I stand, which is pretty big now. Around us, close to us, there are people with badges showing their names, others with EAPPI waistcoats, others with CPT peaked caps (Christian Peacemakers Teams). They are Israelis and internationals from different human rights organisations that have come out alerted by my screams.

I then see D. and it turns out they have stolen his camera too. We go up to the flat and recap. Three cameras stolen. My screams have alerted the whole neighbourhood and everyone, including Palestinians, internationals from other groups and Israeli activists, have come out to the street. A. and D. think that it was a good thing that I alerted the neighbourhood. A few Israelis actually confronted the soldiers, then they were detained and someone else called the police.

The border police have arrived to the street now and the officers are very angry about those detentions. Some of the other activists think that we should report the thefts to the police but S. and D. say that they know, from experience, that if we speak to the police, we will be arrested:

"It always happens when they [the Israeli police] intervene in conflicts between the soldiers and us. If we go to the police station to report this or to ask for our cameras back, they will arrest us."

Even so, some people consider the possibility of speaking to them and reporting the theft of our cameras, since it is an illegal act - the soldiers can detain us, facilitate our arrest by the police, but never take our property. In theory they should be "done" for this. But people who have been here longer know from experience that, once we attempt to talk to the police, we will be arrested and probably deported. And we know that anyone who has been arrested or deported will never be allowed entry into Israel again, and by extension, by virtue of their illegal occupation, into Palestine either.

Those who are planning to stay in Palestine for a few more months think that, if one of us is to go to the police station, it should be someone who is planning to leave for home shortly, and not them. The logic is that, if they are deported now, they lose the months they had available, to spend them either in jail waiting for the deportation or at home once deported, but if we are planning to go home soon anyway, then we are not losing that much.

Then some of the "short-timers" think that it should be someone who has already been arrested who should go, since they are not going to be allowed back in the country anyway, because they have already been arrested once. The criterion for this is not the few more months that someone is planning to stay, but the few more times that some people are planning to come back.

In the end no one goes. We all want to stay here for as long as we can and we all want to come back.

N. calls IDF various times and finally the woman on the phone says that they will give the cameras back to us in a few minutes. An hour passes and the cameras are still stolen. More calls ensue.

Still trembling and trying to fix my glasses, I ask M. and C. where they were while I was struggling with the soldiers.

"We were right next to you, but just before the soldiers grabbed you all at once, another one came, a lot bigger than the rest, and he grabbed us both at once, from our clothes, like this", and he raises both his fists, spreading his arms, "and lifted us from the ground, and he kept us like that until they got your camera".

M. says he also had to fight with a soldier who wanted to steal his camera. However after just the first attempt he realised that he would try again and he changed the tape.

An hour later I am still trembling. I can not help but feel guilty and utterly useless and dumb:

"How could I be so stupid? Did I not see that they would not stop until they got my camera? Why did it not occur to me to run to the flat as quickly as I could and hide the tape, the camera?"

Second thoughts:

"Well, maybe that would have been worse, maybe then the soldiers would have raided the flat looking for it."

"No, that is unlikely".

S. tells me that this is the second camera he has had here. The previous one was smashed by a settler who was enraged because S. had taken a picture of him while he was beating up a Palestinian man in the street. But the fact that what has happened to me is not extraordinary at all, but rather quite common, is by no means a consolation, and it does not make me feel any less stupid. I hide my face in my hands.

"Don't torment yourself. Try to relax", he tells me.

Two hours after we had one photo camera and two video cameras stolen we receive a call to tell us that they are "available". If we want them, we have to go to the soldiers' post to get them, from the hands of the same soldiers that have stolen them from us. It will be some time before I can stomach approaching a soldier, so I ask that someone else goes.

A. offers. From one of our windows we see him go up to the kind of tent the soldiers are in. He stands there for a few seconds, maybe talking to the soldier inside. Then we see a camera coming out from the tent, and the hand holding it. A. grabs it. Then another camera. Then another one. Then he walks back to the flat where we are.

As we had guessed, all tapes have been erased. Instead of a few bad shots, there are wonderful views of green military trousers, black boots and an engine - a green one. The footage of the man unloading and loading his donkey, among others, is gone too.

They have also emptied the batteries completely, so our cameras will need to stay at home being charged for the rest of the day. In any case I do not feel like going out and even less so with a camera. My legs are still trembling against my will and my whole body is aching. D. for his part entertains himself recording everything he can from the window in his room.

After an hour or so, he tells me:

"Could you go downstairs and tell A. to go up to the soldier? A bunch of settler kids are throwing stones at a Palestinian house". While he says this I go to his window. Indeed, a bunch of kids from about five to ten years old are grabbing some stones bigger than their heads and throwing them against a Palestinian house right below the garden where they are.

I run down the stairs, arrive where A. and V. are, I point to the kids for them and we all go to speak to the nearest soldier. By the time we reach him the kids have stopped their pastime. But as we arrive again next to the path with the razor wire we see two little Palestinian girls waiting for someone to open a gap so that they can get to their house. Only one of them wants to go through, the other one has come to accompany her to see the soldier. They talk to them and they look like they do hope to get to their home the short way instead of walking for twenty minutes.

"Why can't she get through?"

"She has no identification, so I cannot check that she lives there."

"I know her and I know that she lives in that house you can see there."

"No one can pass."

"Yes they can, there is a court order (from the authorities of your country, Israeli) that says that this path must be open."

"Eh?"

We explain in simple English:

"An Israeli judge, from the High Court, has ordered: this path must be open."

"I don't know anything about that, my orders are 'no one passes', I don't know what you're saying."

The soldier's face looks more and more stupid by the second. A. says to him:

"She is not old enough to have ID, and this should not be closed anyway."

"My orders are not to open, if I can't check that she lives there."

"I know her and she lives there."

"Ok, if you say she is too young to have ID, I believe you, she can go."

And he goes and opens the razor wire, disobeying the orders he says he has.

At dark, when we have "officially" finished "work", we start cooking and we realise that we need some more pasta. I go to the only shop in the neighbourhood that remains open. It only has sweets, bread, pasta packets and little more, but at least it is a place where kids can socialise when, for instance, the soldiers of the day feel like stealing their ball.

The shop is full of kids now. As I enter, they all look at me and laugh, some scream with their arms stretched out, imitating my screams and my posture when the soldiers took my camera.

I smile and think: "Kids". After the jokes, some of them shake my hand, others simply lower their heads as if showing their respect.

I buy the pasta and the bigger boy, the one who did not want the others to speak to me the other day, approaches me and says, in English: "I'm sorry". I say everything is ok and I leave, while the screams and the laughs continue behind me again. My body is not aching any more and I smile.

Seventh Sunday - **Mini-kristallnachtt**

D. is leaving for a few days. He is going to see R., at the jail that Israel has next to the border with Egypt, in the most southern point of the country, on the other side of the desert. R. is going to be deported for staying in the country while he was waiting for his appointment to renew his visa and helping out the girls in this neighbourhood, like we are doing now. I will leave before D. returns from visiting R. so we exchange addresses and say our goodbyes. I take a few hours off and I decide to do some tourism, like I did in Jerusalem.

I again go through the same checkpoint I used when I first came here, only in the other direction. The soldier outside, before entering the coffin-checkpoint, asks me:

"Why are you here?"

I remain without answering for a few seconds, trying to figure out whether he actually means to ask this question or he is trying to be funny, and to give myself a bit of time, I answer:

"Because I want to get to the other side.".

He insists, with his quite basic English:

"No, why you are here, in Palestine, in Hebron."

Still not knowing what he really is after, I answer:

"Because I defend life."

"Really!" he asks, sounding completely uninterested. He looks at me and I answer:

"Look that way (I indicate to the Israeli settlement), everything is death, silence. Listen to that other side (I indicate to the free part of Hebron, at the other side of the coffin-checkpoint), you can hear life. You bring death to Palestine. Where there are no settlers nor soldiers, there is life and joy, where there are Israelis, there is only silence and death."

"I agree", he says. So I really do not know what this guy is about. I leave him there with his machine gun, and I go off.

I get through the checkpoint that feels rather like a coffin with mirrors and as soon as I get to the end of the empty street I truly feel like I have just got out of a tomb where I was buried alive, and I am suddenly back in the noisy, blinding and colourful world of the living. It is actually strange to get out to the rest of Hebron and see that there is normal life there, that constant humiliations and hatred do not need to be the normal way of life. The street is full of contrasts and colours - and noise. Above all, the noise.

It is as if the city that is still allowed to have some life in it wanted to remind the strangled city, by means of that noise, that there is still life on this side, that there is still hope, that the dying city is neither alone nor forgotten.

I turn right towards the mosque, and again I see, on my right, a high, boring, daunting wall - "the" wall - and a few watch towers with soldiers inside. I then remember that behind this wall and the towers is the illegal Israeli settlement whose inhabitants so terrorise our neighbours.

The Palestinians I see on my way seem to ignore this wall. It looks like they are used to it, maybe resigned themselves to it. What can not be ignored is that the streets become more and more silent and sepulchral as one approaches the old city, even on this "side", where the Palestinian authority is supposed to be in charge, even though there are no checkpoints or soldiers in the streets. There is a point when it actually "is" like on the other side of the wall, with all the shops closed and with stars of David painted on the doors. I am approaching Ibrahim's mosque and Abraham's synagogue.

At the end of the street there is a kind of grille exactly like the one in Qalandia and other checkpoints, only even smaller and in the middle of the city. There are soldiers guarding it, on this side and the other. Some are inside cabins from which they activate the revolving gate made of railings. Just looking at it from the outside, I can guess that it must be really claustrophobic when passing through that revolving gate.

The gate has three "wings" that leave just enough space between them for one not-too-fat person, not even for one person plus baggage. On each side there are round walls made of iron bars, so that the "wings" of the gate go between those bars. If the gate gets blocked, there is really no gap through which to get out, either through the sides or over the top. Fig 18

Fig 18: Checkpoint inside the Mosque in Hebron

Behind me there are about twenty little girls in school uniforms accompanied by some teachers. Once at the other side, I stay discreetly a few metres away from the gate to see if they will make the little girls go through the same process. They do.

I stay where I am for a few more minutes and I see what I was secretly fearing but wished were not true. After the little girls go, a man comes. When he is in the claustrophobic cubicle, suddenly the gate gets blocked and the man stays trapped there for a few seconds. The man looks stunned. He stares at the iron bars around him, so close to his body, and tries to make the gate revolve again. In the end the gate gives in and the man can get out. I stay a bit more until several men get through and I observe that the same thing is done to various other men, at random.

No one says a thing, all happens in silence. But it is obvious that the blocking of the gate is not coincidence and it is controlled by some soldier in some sentry box. Thinking of the whole exercise, it seems to be useless if it is "used" to spot potential terrorists, but very effective if the objective is one more humiliation.

I take some pictures and go on walking towards the temple of various faiths. There are quite a few Palestinian people queueing to enter the mosque. I join the queue but the soldiers "in charge" tell me with signs that I can jump the queue.

I enter a small room where there are again various soldiers with their huge machine guns on their chests and they ask me whether I am a Jew, a Christian or a Muslim. They also ask lots of other questions and I ask:

"Why are you asking me so many questions?", because this is the first time I am asked so many questions at once. The soldier gets cocky at once and, with a commanding gesture of his hand, snaps:

"Right. Passport."

I try to disengage myself from a confrontation that would be all too familiar and remind myself that I am a foreign tourist visiting the fourth most important holy site for Islam and the second one for Judaism. So although I am naturally surprised at the intense questioning, I am also naturally used to being asked for my passport. I hand it to the soldier, he looks at it, he hands it back without a word and I mumble:

"What now?" expecting an answer like "You are detained", or "arrested", or something of the like. Instead, he tells me:

"You have to wait." He looks at another soldier in a small office separated from us by some glass doors. That soldier is on the phone. I look away, at the different walls, as if already enjoying the building I came here to visit, and at some point the first soldier says:

"You can pass."

He points to a door and I go through it. I am then in a narrow and claustrophobic corridor. At the beginning of this corridor there is a door on one side, with Hebrew characters painted on it, and a small window that lets you see a bit of what is on the other side of it. I see a man in a black hat, glasses and ringlets on

121

both sides of his face. He looks at me in a not-too-friendly way. I continue walking down the corridor and I realise that I am not going to be allowed to visit the Jewish part of the building.

The corridor ends at an enormous room where there are two Palestinians looking at me, smiling. A third one, also smiling, approaches me, telling me with gestures to come in. However he is not pointing at the next door as I would have expected, but at a closet next to that door. He opens the door of the closet and I see a lot of capes hung from hooks, all with a hood, of very similar sizes, and all of the very same very dark brown colour.

He grabs one of the capes and helps me to put it on. It feels as if I were suddenly in a cave, only really small, with the walls of the cave made of smooth material and sticking to my body, but a cave all the same. I am also invited to leave my shoes in a corner set aside for it. Barefoot, I enter through the door that the seated men now indicate to me.

The room in which I enter is a room dedicated to prayers. It is divided into two "sections". One looks like a wide corridor that goes from the door I have just used to get in here right to another door at the other side of the room, in front of me. To the right of the corridor is the wall, and on the left there is a much wider section covered with what looks like a thick carpet, or maybe various layers of carpets. The carpeted floor is about five centimetres higher than the floor of the corridor, which has no carpet. The carpeted part is the main part of the room and has many columns; the stone part is rather just a corridor between both doors, and it does not have a single column. There is no furniture, neither benches nor chairs, to sit on.

There is an intense atmosphere of meditation, and having my head covered with this brown hood, seeing everything through the opening that the hood allows, contributes to this feeling of meditation and smallness. I can only see men, all in an attitude of meditation, knelt or seated on the floor, although they are all wearing street clothes.

A question crosses my mind: Why would it be unsuitable to help the men have this feeling too, with a cape and a hood? Although, the truth is, I do not feel uncomfortable with it. I feel privileged to be able to visit a temple dedicated to a faith to which in principle I do not belong. In fact it makes me wonder why there is not this custom in other religions too, to put something special on at the door, to become fully conscious of just how special the site you are going to enter is.

I kneel on the step that is formed by the height difference between the two sections and all that has happened in the past weeks, mainly the last one, comes right into my head at once. I end up recalling that, throughout History, so many of the greatest crimes of Humanity continue to be committed "in the Name of God".

My hood insists on falling off my head and I end up not caring. It falls on my back again but this time I do not put it back on. No one seems to notice; nobody says anything.

Finally I leave the carpeted zone, I give back the cape, I put my shoes back on and go out back to the street.

Once outside, the waiting queue that I have seen before is now shorter, but a few boys I saw when I jumped the queue are still here, waiting. I ask them if they are detained and one says no, but adds that they have been trying to enter the mosque for two hours now and they are not allowed in. I ask the Israeli soldier and he answers reluctantly that he is waiting for some type of confirmation from somewhere. I wish them luck and I continue towards the street, but it seems that they have given up and they come with me. I realise they communicate by signs. The one that speaks to me says they are deaf-mute and he is the activities supervisor. Today they had wanted to go to the mosque together but they have not been allowed in. Another humiliation.

K. phones to ask me to come home as soon as I can because a "mini-kristallnachtt" has happened. When I arrive home we all go to the house of a neighbour to take pictures of the damage some settlers have done to it during my absence. After hearing the noise of breaking glass, they just found all the windows broken and glass pieces all over the floor. The vandals left behind the iron bar they have smashed all the house windows with.

Fig 19: Water drum with bullets

EIGHTH WEEK

Eigth Monday - **From Hebron to Kawawis**

Today is my last day in Hebron and I do a "tour" around the house where we are staying as a goodbye. It is a neighbours' building and the most interesting part of it is the flat roof.

We can see the top of other roofs from here, and some are higher up than this one; all are Palestinian. On one of those higher roofs there is an outpost of the Israeli army, with its sentry box and a kind of curtain that looks like a fishing net, only it is of a military green colour. K. explains that the roof is illegally occupied, but with no recognised authority to appeal to, there is absolutely nothing that the family living there can do to try and stop it.

K. also points to a pair of water drums left there in a corner, on our roof. They are the drums containing the water that is supplied to all the neighbours of this building. Both have holes which have obviously been caused by bullets. K. explains that the soldiers and the settlers seem to be terribly bored and sometimes they entertain themselves shooting at the drums, making them useless. The families living in the houses then lose their water supply for days or weeks, however long it takes them to replace the drums. Fig 19

Looking down on the street below we can see, apart from the sentry boxes, something we do not tend to pay much attention to when we are at their level, but which from here is so distinctive: the street dug up just next to the entrance of the houses. K. explains that it is common practice, to remove the pavement to humiliate them just a bit more, and make their lives just a little bit more impossible. It is done with one of those machines that in a normal country are used when a pipe below the asphalt needs to be repaired. Here the machine arrives, digs up the street, repairs nothing and leaves the street paving destroyed for good, leaving the inhabitants of that house embittered, having to climb over the debris whenever they need to leave and enter their house. Sometimes the family can afford the luxury of fixing it. Sometimes, they can not. Fig 20

After the morning shift and breakfast, I go to the lower street on my way to the tomb-with-mirrors checkpoint, and towards the live part of the city. I walk down with S., who will be at the spot where I have been most of my time here.

There is a child detained at the checkpoint and we ask the soldier why. He tells us he was carrying a knife with a six centimetre long blade and he has to detain him because Palestinians are not allowed to walk with weapons. We wait for ten minutes and, since he does not release him, we ask him to show us the knife. The soldier shows us a plastic bag. Inside there is, in fact, a kitchen knife, inside the package where it is sold in the shop. The blade must be three centimetres long at most. S. tells the soldier that it is clear that this boy comes from an errand for his mother, who must have asked him to buy this, and that, if it is necessary, we will bring the mother here. The boy nods, looking down. The soldier releases the boy and when we are far away from the checkpoint he tells us that he has done it on purpose, to get arrested and then taken to the prison where his father is, to be with him.

There are more soldiers than usual on the street today. I see a military vehicle loaded with them, on the very street where Palestinians are not allowed to ride other than bikes or donkeys. The soldiers stare at us from the rear window of their vehicle and smile with sarcasm as they wave us goodbye, making visual references to the incident with my camera.

From here I am going to Kawawis, as suggested by J.

Sometimes it sounds like "Kawawis", other times like "Kaa-ou-ees" and other times like "Kwees", depending on who pronounces it. It is too small a village to start asking for a service from here; I need to ask for one to Yatta and then change there.

Fig 20 Street dug up

My first "stop" is the centre of Hebron. Once in the taxi zone, I ask for a service to Yatta and a man who speaks English answers with a question:

"You are going to Kawawis, aren't you?"

"How do you know?"

"All the foreigners that ask for Yatta, are going to Kawawis".

Of course. I am not the first one and will not be the last one. He gets me a taxi and I leave.

The journey is incident free; there is not even any checkpoint that would make us get off the taxi. Until we approach Yatta. An Israeli settler drives his car like mad, not respecting the Palestinian "stop" sign, almost killing a bunch of Palestinian school girls and then waving furiously at a Palestinian driver who had actually stopped to avoid a crash.

Once in the main street of Yatta, which is full of Palestinian boys and men, I go from shop to shop buying food, trying to buy enough for the three days that I am staying there. I have been told that Kawawis is only a handful of houses, with no shops.

A man with a beard approaches me:

"To Kawawis? Yes? I take you". By the time he finishes the sentence a circle of about ten men has formed around us. The guy tells me that he will take me for twenty five shekels. I was told it would be about five, so I tell him that I'll think about it, but it's not like I have lots of options, since it is the only taxi that I can see around here. I buy some more food, which he helps me buy and carry, and we get in his van. It is the first time in Palestine that I get in a taxi on my own.

He takes me through roads full of irregular piles of stones and roadblocks, which are basically pairs of stone blocks of about one or two cubic metres, planted in the middle of the roads in order to make motor transport impossible. He can hardly drive the van through them. At one point he shouts above the deafening noise of the engine and the stones under the tyres:

"This road - destroyed by Israel!" Which is a very useful observation because, without this information, it would be easy to simply assume that no road ever existed, nor the intention to build one, and what we are following is just the trail of previous drivers, or that someone started to build a road but then half way through these stones fell on it and they could not finish it off...

The road is cut short by another road, this one perfectly asphalted, and the van has to stop here. It is like most Israeli roads I have seen, blocking Palestinian roads, leaving people isolated. It seems that this one did go all the way to Kawawis before, because a stony trail similar to this one can be seen on the other side of the Israeli road, all the way to a bunch of houses that I imagine is Kawawis. Now Kawawis is totally isolated and it is only possible to get there on foot.

The taxi driver starts to walk with me but when he sees that I am walking straight to the Israeli road he apologises:

"Dangerous", he says. I perfectly understand. He can not get anywhere near it. As the potential terrorist that he is, and since Palestinian life is not worth very much here, his mere presence near an Israeli highway would amply justify a shot in his head.

So there I go, with my hair down as "proof" that I am not a Palestinian, therefore not a terrorist, therefore they can not kill me and easily get away with it. Once on the verge of the road I should see L., who should get this same taxi to get to Yatta.

Trucks, big coaches, cars and some military vehicles travel at high speed on this road that is not cut short by anything or anybody. I imagine their passengers must wonder where the hell I have come out from and where the hell I am going. I walk on the verge looking for L., crossing it a few times.

L. and I finally see each other in the distance and run to meet. She points to the house where I will stay and gives me the key. I take her to the taxi and she gets in, with all her stuff. The taxi sets off back to Yatta and I am left alone in what feels like the middle of nowhere. There is no indication of life, apart from the tracks of the taxi on the stony trail we came on.

I finally cross the road for the last time for a few days, and after walking for about ten minutes I arrive near a bunch of buildings no higher than two metres each. The biggest one is a dark grey square; the others look like igloos made of stones. As I go round one of these "igloos" I see two women, one of them very old and the other one younger, and a man, whose age could be between the ages of the two women. They are sitting on a kind of platform, drinking tea and looking at me. It looks like they were waiting for me. They welcome me, with the very few words that they can say in English, and they give me the sweetest tea I have ever tasted. So here I stay, sitting on the floor of this platform, my backpack and my shopping on the ground.

Thanks to their great efforts to speak in English to me, I learn that the oldest woman and the man are a married couple and the youngest woman, H., is their unmarried daughter. H. appears to be about fifty years old. When she smiles she shows off some gold teeth and also some gaps. She says she is thirty.

After two little glasses of tea I point to my things and the key I have been given. They, in turn, point to the igloo I have just come round from and they stay there, while I get into the igloo-house for which I have been given the key. Like the other igloos, it is made of stones, one on top of the other, making up a circular wall, with a canvas covering the only resulting room. There are no windows; the only source of natural light is the gap of the entrance when the door is open. There is also a light bulb hanging from the ceiling, but there is electricity only for a few hours each night.

Almost all the "houses" look like this one from the outside, so I imagine they will be similar inside too. This one has several mats and blankets, just enough for two or three people to sleep here. L. has left some bread and biscuits. Next to the food there is a notebook where people who have been here before me have been writing down "incidents". I sit down to read. They are all about settlers abusing the Palestinians and soldiers not doing anything about it; one that stands out involves settlers burning a whole field of olive trees.

People have signed what they have written and I recognise some of the names. They are people I have been with, in other places in Palestine, and I can imagine them here, in this very house, or on the platform having tea, or getting up at six in the morning, as they write, in order to accompany the older man with the sheep flock. It almost feels like they are all here with me now.

I finish reading the notebook and as I get to the door to go out I notice the poster on it, hand-made, which is a map explaining the area. Fig 21

There are three settlements. Facing the valley, with my back to the road for Israeli settlers, one is on my right, another is on my left, both on mountain tops, and the third one is also towards the right but behind, at the other side of the road, and it can not be seen.

The scrawls between the two settlements and Kawawis on the hand-made map indicate an olive grove and a family's house, there alone, facing both settlements. If I had come with someone else, one of us would have gone to visit that family so that they do not feel so alone in the face of danger. But as I have come on my own, instructions are to stay near the bigger group of houses. I should not go out on visits outside of this central group of houses and I can not go to the fields with the flocks in the morning, as other internationals have done before me. I must

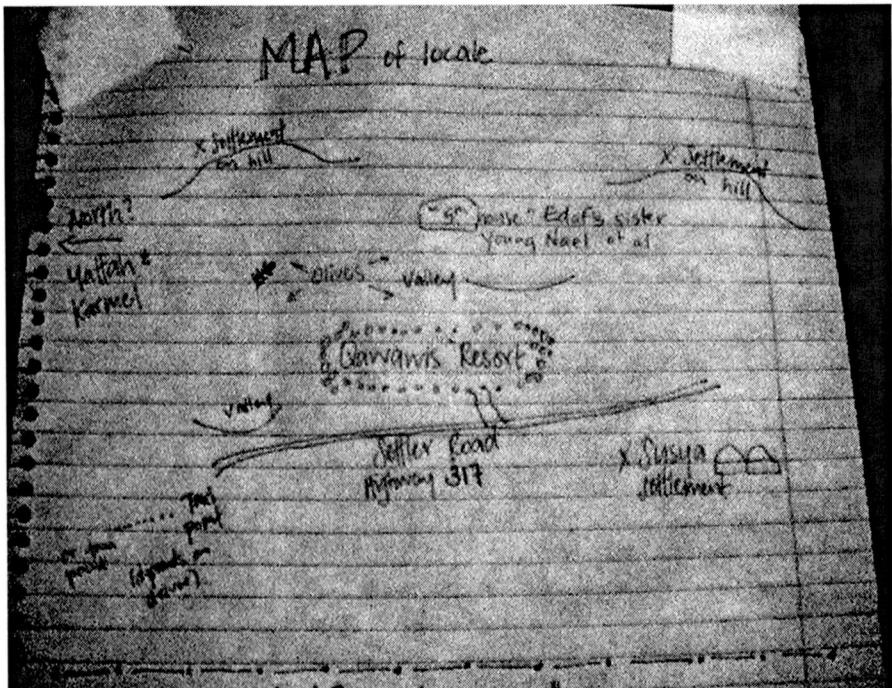

Fig 21 Map of Kawawis

128

stay here to be found easily. In any case, those outings would have been made by a male, not a female volunteer, but that is another story.

As I leave the "house" I find H. and a young girl sitting on its doorstep, outside. The girl can speak English a bit better than H., and says she is her niece. I invite them to eat with me but they do not understand. H. goes away and her niece stays, and I invite her to come in by signs. I begin to eat and I give her some food, and we eat something together. She asks me for some bread to take to her brother, I give her some, and she asks for some more, now for her sister. I also offer her hummus and she asks me for some biscuits. After a little while she puts a few biscuits in her pockets and she leaves, with the hummus sandwich in one hand and bread alone in the other, and I am left with the certainty that these people are starving.

Because of the scarcity of food here we are told that we should eat on our own instead of accepting their invitation to eat their food with them, so I continue eating on my own. Shortly afterwards H. comes, telling me, with signs, to go to her house with her. I point at my food and she helps me gather it. It is normally not appropriate to bring food to a house where you are invited; it is considered offensive. It would be like saying to them that they are not worth enough to feed you. But this family receives it with a smile and we all eat their food and mine.

When we finish eating, and after tea, H. does the washing up with a remarkably small amount of water, a strange scourer and a bar of olive oil soap.
I get up in order to go to my cave to sleep but they are not going to allow me:

"Two, good, one, not good" H. says, which I guess means that it is ok for two to sleep in the little house but not for one alone. And, although I feel quite uncomfortable with the offer, I do not feel at all like staying on my own in that cave, aware that the soldiers in the sentry box on the top of the hill know that I am the only foreigner here.

So we go to the small house-cave where I am supposed to be staying and we bring the mattresses and blankets that I will be using to their house.

The room where we are going to sleep looks a bit like a multi-purpose room. There are square holes in the wall acting as windows. No frame, no glass. There is also a pile of mattresses in a corner and they take them, one by one, distributing them around the room, against the walls. A boy who looks about twenty years old has turned up, although, knowing how people grow old faster here, he might as well be fifteen or less. He is also a nephew of H. She is always smiling at me, always trying to make as much conversation as we can with our more than limited language skills. She has now started to say that I am her "sister".

H. says her prayers and, again smiling, lies down to sleep on a mattress next to me, wearing her hijab. I look at her expecting to see her hair but no, she does not take her headscarf off. She goes to sleep with exactly the same clothes she wears around the house and surroundings. Thinking of it, I have not seen a single piece of furniture in this house, so chances are none of them have any other clothes than the ones they have on.

Eighth Tuesday - **Flour USAID**

I wake up at eight o'clock in the morning as the sun comes in full swing into the room through the glassless windows. The couple seem to have got up already; their mattress is no longer there. Their grandson is gone too. I remember then what I read yesterday in the log book: that they go to walk the sheep at about six in the morning.

H. is saying her prayers standing up, with her eyes closed and swinging her body from time to time. When she finishes praying we put all the mattresses and blankets in the corner where they seem to be kept and I help her prepare breakfast, which consists of tea made with herbs collected in the area.

Stacked against one of the walls there is a pile of sacks full of what turns out to be flour, with the word USAID written on each of them. When we finish breakfast H. grabs one of them and spills some flour on an old sack opened on the floor. She then grabs another sack and spills some more flour. This one is darker. She is going to make bread with plain and wholemeal flour mixed together.

When she finishes, she puts the bread away and I help her clean the floor where she has been working. Her parents come into the house and we have tea. After a bit more chilling out time we share our food and then the father leaves.

Eighth Wednesday - **Visit day**

A lot of grandchildren of H.'s mother come to see her today. They had to come on foot, crossing the road that functions as a wall. The older boys just say hello and some of them stare at me. The younger children ignore me and kiss their grandmother in veneration, first on her cheek, then on her hand, and then they bend their heads to put their forehead on that same hand that they have just kissed. Then the grandmother asks them who they are, they answer and the grandmother nods in recognition. Then the ritual is repeated by all the grandchildren who have come to see her, one by one.

In the middle of the visit, some men come and stay standing, talking. I look at H. and she tells me they are also cousins of hers and grandchildren of her mother, visiting. They talk amongst themselves in Arabic until one of them looks at me and says:

"Settlers."

I get up thinking that they are now going to guide me to wherever the local settlers are causing problems. With his basic English, he says:

"No, not now. Days ago."

I sit back on the floor.

The situation in Kawawis is very similar to that of Yanoun. The settlers harassed this village so badly a few years ago, the villagers just ran away, and only agreed to come back on condition that there would be internationals here continuously.

When the visitors leave, the older woman goes to the room where we all sleep. She goes there and prays five times each day. Each time, H. stays with me, and when the mother returns, she goes, in such a way that I am never left on my own.

Eighth Thursday - **The journalist**

I receive a call saying that E., will be coming today for a visit. E. is an Israeli activist who comes here regularly to get information about incidents that need to be reported, and generally to give moral support.

E. comes with an Irish journalist who asks me lots of questions while E. talks to the villagers in Arabic. It is clear that the journalist has no idea what this is about. He even asks me if I really feel safe here on my own with so many Palestinians. When I overcome the shock of such a question and manage to understand what he is on about, I answer:

"Look. They venerate us. The only thing that makes me feel unsafe is that outpost there, and the settlers that inhabit the three settlements that we can not see".

He does not even know where the settlements are, why they are there or why we are here.

But he has not come here to find that out or to see what these people's daily lives are like. He has only come here to take pictures of the proof of the incidents H.'s cousin was talking about before, so he interrupts me to ask what I saw when the settlers burnt the olive trees. He only gives me time to tell him that I was not here then, and he turns round in the middle of my sentence, already ignoring me.

E. takes his journalist to the field where the Israeli settlers have recently burned all the olive trees that were a good part of the village's livelihood, and that's the end of this week's visit.

Eighth Friday - **News from Jayyous**

I wake up to find myself on my own, so I just get up and eat some of the food I brought with me as breakfast. I hear the sound of an engine and go to see what it is. Two men, one on foot and another one on a tractor, are spreading seeds on the fields around the village.

I make a point of keeping an eye on them, especially when they work on the land close to the Israeli road I had to cross to come here.

After a few minutes an Israeli military vehicle comes down the road and stops. Before any of the occupants can get off the military vehicle, the Palestinian men get away from the road. This year that patch of land will not grow anything.

I go round the village and a child comes up to me to invite me to his family's home. Indeed the igloo-house is also similar to the internationals' one inside, only this one is crowded. There is a small fire in the middle of the room heating the tea that we all drink. There must be about twenty people here, between the older woman who seems to be the mother and young people of different ages. The oldest one might be twenty. All of them, even the small boy who can not be more than two years old, have a very tanned and hardened skin. They tell me they live in the nearest village with brothers or uncles during the week to go to school and they come back on Fridays to be with their parents. The children leave well before dusk because they can only go back on foot.

I go back to H. and her parents and we go to the cave where they keep the sheep in the cold weather. We gather all the sheep manure and H. puts it in bags. Then we put the bags away for storage. When we finish, I begin to pack because today should be the last day I am here. After eating I receive a call from my re-placement. I grab my backpack and say goodbye, before repeating the scene of the taxi leaving one person and picking up another, only this time it is me leaving.

I am not set to replace anyone from here. I am going to Jerusalem, ready to get on a plane. Not before going through the checkpoints, of course.

In the taxi that I get in Yatta there are three other passengers but we travel in silence. As we approach a flying checkpoint, the passenger sitting next to me looks nervous:

"Can I ask you a favour", he says to me in a low voice. "If they ask us for identification. I have, but at home. Would you tell them that I am with you?"

"Sure. I'll tell them you are my guide".

Luckily, when we get to the checkpoint, the soldier in charge does not make us get out of the taxi. He bends over to look through the passenger window, sees my western face and says "go" with his hand. They have not checked our passports or identification. My "guide" looks relieved.

At the first stop of this taxi, well before Jerusalem, he gets out. I do not understand the words he speaks with the taxi driver but from the way he points at me while talking to him, and the quick glance of the driver, I guess he is going to pay for my fare. I begin to protest but the guy leaves quickly.

"He has paid your fare", says the taxi driver to me. I look at him through the rear window and I see his lips saying:

"Thank you."

The last vehicle I get on is one of those van-taxis that wait to be full before leaving. I look for an empty seat and a familiar voice calls my name. I look at the occupied seats and I spot G., one of the people who stayed with Abu A. after J. and I left Jayyous in O.'s car. I sit down next to him, happy to have someone I know to speak to, and we update each other with our stories.

G. has spent a few months in Jayyous and Abu A. is a friend for life for him now. When J. and I were there, Abu A. had already spent all the money he could get for his wife's jewellery trying to get an injunction to stop the illegal expansion of the already illegal Israeli settlement on his land. The injunction was granted, that we knew. Since then, bulldozers have been on his land, protected by the Israeli army, uprooting his olive trees. Then more bulldozers have been on his land removing soil, preparing the foundations for new buildings. That we knew too.

"He won in court," G. tells me, "but construction is under way. He could go again to court if he had the money, but it would change nothing. They are already building on his land."

I close my eyes, to see more clearly, in my mind, the land I knew in Jayyous, with the olive trees recently uprooted, even with some small olive sprouts coming out of the soil where the trees had stood. And trying to imagine the bulldozers destroying that too.

"Facts on the ground, you know".

Yes, I know.

EPILOGUE

When I came here, I did not know too well what I was coming for. But that is not the most important thing. I have been with people who know only too well what they need us for. And they have put us, they have put me, in the places where I was needed, telling me, on occasions exactly, what needed to be done. They never complained, but I was always aware that they need more nationals from privileged countries. While this humiliating occupation goes on, international solidarity will always be needed.

On occasions, it has been difficult, although the most difficult situations may have been the most trivial, or the ones no one would have expected to be difficult.

Misunderstandings with colleagues were difficult. Misunderstandings with soldiers were frustrating. Fighting with the enemy is not as painful as fighting with your friends.

The "official" reason for writing this is to denounce the situation in Palestine, and thus try and change it, for the better. A more personal reason is to never forget.

I do not want to forget M., who would not stay still while he was explaining things to us. He seemed to be dancing in front of us while he scribbled on the white board, and never stopped smiling.

I do not want to forget N. and her daughters. And her knowledge. And her support.

I do not want to forget R., who always said hello to us in Arabic, maybe in the hope that we would learn it.

I do not want to forget C., from the EAPPI, whom I met in one place and then I saw again in various other places, and it gave us the sensation, amongst so many unknown faces, that we had known each other all our lives.

I do not want to forget all the women who introduced us to their children, and grandchildren, and offered us the little food they had.

Although I did not meet him, I will never forget R., who was arrested during my travels in Palestine, in prison during my stay in Hebron, and deported after I left Palestine.

I do not want to forget D., who visited R. while he could, and who later sent us reports about R. and about himself, and who was himself arrested and then deported. Never to be allowed back again into Israel or Palestine by the Israeli authorities. But, surely, someone else from the rich world who has not been banned yet will fill his place.

The only way to maintain a continuous international presence that will somehow limit and document human rights abuses is to keep a continuous flow of Western people who are prepared to travel to Palestine and spend some time there.

Spending a few weeks, or months, in Palestine, accompanying Palestinians in their everyday struggle and sharing their difficulties, is an act of solidarity that is necessary and also very much appreciated. It is a humanitarian act of sharing the privilege of being a dignified citizen from a respected country with people who do not have that privilege and who are suffering for it.

I take home many things, but one of them is a clear cry for help from the Palestinians to us citizens of rich countries, since our governments are not honouring their good intention declarations. Concretely, they ask us to do however much we can of the following:

go there and share their everyday lives

document it and talk about it back home

boycott Israeli products

Words do not exist to express the gratitude the Palestinians feel when a citizen of a rich country does any one of these things.

CPSIA information can be obtained at www.ICGtesting.com
Printed in the USA
BVOW04s1226210514

354186BV00007B/151/P